FINANCIAL

FREEDOM

IN

THE

FAMINE

by

Marcus A. Beasley

First published by AuthorHouse 07/11/05

ISBN: 1-4184-6089-3 (e-book)
ISBN: 1-4184-2929-5 (Paperback)

Library of Congress Control Number: 2004105021

Printed in the United States of America
Bloomington, IN

This book is printed on acid free paper.

TABLE OF CONTENTS

ACKNOWLEDGMENT PAGE

First and foremost I thank God the Father, Jesus the Christ His Son and the Holy Spirit His Power, for the divine inspiration to share information with His body.

I thank my beautiful wife Denise and my children Paris, Anthony and Christian for bringing so much joy and support to my life.

I thank my parents Jonathan & Clara Beasley for such a wonderful childhood through love and nurturing and my brother Bruce for his competitive nature and ability to motivate.

I thank my spiritual parents Pastors Kenneth & June Robinson for being Godly examples of a Christian lifestyle.

I thank all of the Beasley and Bell families for their faith and trust in the Lord.

I thank all of the friends of my family on St Helena Island S.C.

I thank the class of 1981, the best Beaufort High has ever known.

I thank all of my teachers through the years for helping me learn.

FOREWORD

This book is divinely inspired by the Holy Spirit to restore to the body of believers financial prosperity through the word of the Lord and His natural laws in the earth.

What the Lord is saying to His body is, "We are partners in this covenant. I will not do your part and you cannot do mine." Christians, we have a tremendous responsibility in spreading the good news of the gospel of our Lord and Savior Jesus the Christ. Jesus has commissioned us in Matthew 28:18-20 saying, "All authority has been given to Me in heaven and on earth. Go therefore and make disciples of all the nations, baptizing them in the name of the Father and of the Son and of the Holy Spirit, teaching them to observe all things that I have commanded you; I am with you always, even to the end of the age." Amen. In our world today, there are many means of mass communications to all the nations but it takes MONEY TO SPREAD THE GOSPEL OF CHRIST.

Ecclesiastes 10:19 says, "Money answereth all things in the earth." Therefore, we can logically deduce the significance of money and its role in the body of Christ. However, the world knows more and understands the principles of money and how it works in the earth than the body of Christ. Christ illustrates this in the parable of the unjust steward in Luke 16:8: "For the sons of this world are more shrewd in their generation than the sons of light." If we are to impact the world for Christ we will first have to economically educate the body in creating and building wealth for our families and to financially propel the church as an economic giant in the community.

Money must have been important to Jesus because there are over 2,350 scriptures mentioning money and/or possessions. Also, fifteen percent of the words Jesus spoke involved money or possessions. In addition, of the fifty-four parables that Jesus taught, sixteen of them concerned money.

This book was written to educate the body of Christ economically and to financially empower the church to fulfill its purpose and mission in spreading the gospel to all nations and people.

BUT SEEK YE FIRST THE KINGDOM OF GOD AND HIS RIGHTEOUSNESS AND ALL THESE THINGS WILL BE ADDED UNTO YOU.

FAMINE

God has given His body of believers the victory of economic empowerment through His son Jesus Christ. We are involved in a fixed fight against spiritual wickedness and principalities in which we will be the victors. The Lord God has given us every advantage we would ever need:

1. Psalm 24:1, "the earth is the Lord's and the fullness thereof; the world and they that dwell therein."

2. Genesis 1:26, "Let us make man in our own image, after our likeness: and let them have DOMINION over the fish of the sea, and over the fowl of the air, and over the cattle, and over all the earth, and over every creeping thing that creepeth upon the earth."

3. Psalms 115:16, "the heaven, even the heavens, are the Lord's; but the earth hath He given to the children of men."

4. Deuteronomy 8:18, "for it is He that giveth thee power to get wealth."

God tells us that the earth is His, we are made in His image, He puts us here to dominate and He gives us power to get wealth. What a deal we have. Look at the last deal of the fixed fight. God tells us that He gives us the power to get wealth which suggest that we have a responsibility. He did not say that He gives us wealth but the power to get wealth. Have you tapped into your wealth power? This book will show you how to tap into this power even in the famine.

From 2000–03 in the United States alone, millions of people have already experienced a famine. Government spending has created a deficit in excess of $450 billion dollars. Over a million Americans have faced loss of employment, forced home foreclosure and bankruptcy. The Dow, S&P 500 and Nasdaq plummeted causing enormous losses in retirement accounts. Further, corporate CEOs and CFOs defrauded employees and investors so badly that consumer expectation lowered tremendously. Most states are broke or in serious financial difficulty.

In comparison, however, if we look at the late 1990s our economy experienced a tremendous economic boom. For the first time in history the government had a plan in place to balance the federal budget; this, coupled with low unemployment, high consumer expectation and tremendous gains in the Dow, S&P 500 and Nasdaq, catapulted the economy into economic prosperity.

As clearly reflected here, our economy works in cycles. We must therefore educate ourselves and understand why and how our economy works. God gives us a clear-cut example of this in Genesis 41: 26-36 when Joseph interprets the dream of Pharaoh. Joseph's plan was to store up one fifth of the food for seven years during times of prosperity. This would allow the land of Egypt to have food in the time of famine.

Just as God prepared the land of Egypt to experience economic freedom in the midst of a famine, He wants to prepare you too. By reading and applying the simple principles set forth in the upcoming chapters you to will be able to live without lack and experience financial freedom in the famine.

CHAPTER 1

THE WORLD SYSTEM VS. GOD'S WORD

Do your finances represent Jesus on the cross or Jesus sitting at the right hand of God? Is the world or the Word of God making your financial decisions? Are your current economic circumstances the product of instant gratification, or do they represent faith in God who says in His word, "Blessed are those who do not see and yet believe"?

The answers to these questions and many others are discussed in great length and depth to strengthen the Body of Christ financially.

TRIUNE NATURE OF A SOVERIGN GOD

Psalms 24:1 says "The Earth is the Lord's and the fullness thereof, the world and those who dwell therein.". When we look deeper into what the Holy Scripture is saying, we see God's nature in the financial structure of our economy. The scripture implies God as Triune in nature: the Father, the Son and the Holy Spirit. In addition God identifies Himself as the God of Abraham, Isaac and Jacob. Herein should we expand our knowledge of economics and the impact it has on us as a body of believers and thus our ability to be ambassadors on the earth for Christ.

When we look at the economic structure in our economy, we should note and understand God's presence in our markets. First, let us look at the **three** main barometers that govern the stock markets: **Dow Jones, Nasdaq and S&P 500**. In addition there are **three** main sectors in the economy: **health care, financial services and science & technology**. We also see God's involvement in the **three** cycles in the economy: **stocks/bonds, real estate and cash equivalents**. God does not stop there; there are **three** asset classes of stocks: **large, mid and small cap**. God allowed **three** indexes that govern the **three** asset classes: **S&P 500 Index (large cap) Midcap 400 Index (midcap) and Russell 2000 Index (small cap).** The Lord gave us **three** main economic indicators to warn us of a pending recession: **unemployment numbers, manufacturing numbers and consumer expectation numbers.** We as believers must understand that God has put His sovereign nature in every facet of our economic structure and has divinely orchestrated its direction. However, it is our responsibility to educate ourselves about God's system and how to implement what we have learned.

FLESH VS. SPIRIT

When God created man His desire was to have a Spirit controlled mind that controls his natural members. However, after the fall of Adam man's flesh controlled his mind and the law of sin dominated his nature. Paul wrote in Romans 7:23, "But I see another law in my members, warring against the law of my mind, and bringing me into captivity to the law of sin which is in my members." What does this have to do with our finances?

EVERYTHING. We were born into sin and shaped in iniquity. Therefore, when we were young and impressionable the world programmed our minds and shaped our financial paths. The world made our financial decisions and forced us into negative circumstances because of those worldly decisions. The world has programmed us to claim zero exemptions on our paychecks; what we are telling the government to do is take the highest tax possible as a twelve-month loan and give the money back to us at a 0% interest rate when we file our taxes. We go all year struggling to make ends meet to receive a refund in a lump sum only to purchase items that will depreciate in value. We should know that we can claim up to eight exemptions on our pay. Each exemption adds $64 to our pay.

In addition, the world has kept us ignorant regarding economics and finances in our families. We have not been taught to save or the significance of a good credit report and its importance. Why is it that gospel radio stations promote **cash-to-you leasing centers as financial institutions in our neighborhoods?** These cash-to-you leasing centers offer money until your next paycheck. But they are charging you 24% interest on their loan to you. STOP IT. Rent-to-own centers in our communities offer brand name merchandise on credit and charge us astronomical interest; they make it attractive by charging us "only" $10 to $12 a week. In addition, they allow us to pay for twenty-four to thirty-six months, but by the time we finish paying for a $199 VCR we will have paid twice the amount it would cost to buy it with cash. Also, in my home state of South Carolina there are businesses that will allow us to borrow money on our car titles as collateral. We don't understand that we are giving ownership of our vehicle to a business that knows 50% of the people will not be able to pay off the loan. **STOP IT. STOP IT.** There was a study done regarding the African American dollar in 2000; our spending habits are economic heaven for businesses and a financial nightmare for our families. Between 1998 and 1999 we increased our spending 40% on **MAGAZINES.** Our income in 2001 increased to $572.1 billion; we spent $25 billion on **CLOTHING,** $53 billion on **FOOD,** $2 billion on **ENTERTAINMENT** and under $1 billion for **BOOKS** and **HEALTH CARE.** It is astonishing that we spend more on material possessions that decrease in value as opposed to educating ourselves and staying in good health. We are exploited by every nationality on earth because of our buying habits. Our communities have nail shops and cleaners owned by other nationalities and races, restaurants, pawn shops, cash leasing centers, liquor stores and apparel stores with brand name merchandise. We are not the owners of any of these businesses in our communities. If we are, we then take our business to the other nationality groups. In our communities the dollar changes hands only once before it leaves our communities. In other communities the average is four times before it leaves their communities. Wake up; we need to keep this money in our communities to create jobs and become a self-sufficient society of people.

In every category mentioned above we are #1 on spending based on our income to spending percentages. Why? The world promotes spending and debt. There are advertising campaigns designed to specifically target people of color because we are the most loyal people to brand name merchandise and are willing to pay higher prices for the name. My point is the world programs our 18 billion brain cells in creating a bondage situation called **DEBT.** The world's decision making creates negative circumstances that impacts our lives after we have repented and been converted into the faith of Jesus the Christ; we then enter the body of Christ with a bad credit report and in debt. How can we effectively represent Christ in the earth when the children of darkness are financially wiser than the children of light? WHO IS MAKING YOUR FINANCIAL DECISIONS?

The world (Satan)	VS.	THE LORD GOD
flesh		SPIRIT
fear (instant gratification)		FAITH
goat		SHEEP
comfortable		UNCOMFORTABLE
indebtedness		DEBT FREEDOM
receiving		TITHING
religion (tradition)		RELATIONSHIP
ignorance		KNOWLEDGE, WISDOM, UNDERSTANDING
job		ENTREPRENEUR

FEAR VS. FAITH

Fear is the world's best friend and the believer's worst enemy; the world is the ultimate promoter of fear. Fear is defined as apprehension or dread of impending danger or trouble; the world has programmed us from birth that our fears and apprehensions will serve us well. Fear is a trait in which it deprives the believer from reaching his/her potential in God. Fear causes us not to obey God's purpose for our lives. For example, you may have a burning desire to own your own business but because of the fear of economic circumstances you decide not to pursue what God has instilled within you to do. The world may tell you that one in two small businesses fail in the first year and the current marketplace conditions is not conducive to following your dreams in business. Therefore, the world and its system has penetrated your mind and the decisions you are making are flesh-controlled. If your flesh is controlling your mind, then the world is creating negative circumstances; these circumstances breed fear, and then your decisions are made because of the fear factor. Look at the great men and women in the Bible. They too had to overcome the fear factor in order for God to effectively use them. Moses, who grew up in the court of Pharaoh, had slurred speech but overcame the fear factor to deliver God's people.

Joshua experienced all of the fears and apprehensions of Moses, yet he took God's people into the promised land. As a matter of fact God repeatedly had to reinforce Joshua to be strong and of good courage. David had to rise from a mere shepherd boy to king of God's chosen people. David experienced great fear, as evidenced by some of the Psalms, but he overcame the fear factor. Fear hurts the believers the most in the area of finances. Fear causes us not to invest our money in the stock market but keep it in a bank to grow at only 1.9% interest. Fear causes us not to take risks and we know just as in investing that low risk = low returns. In addition, no risk = no returns. Now, let us examine God's answer to fear—FAITH.

FAITH

In Paul's letter to the Hebrews, he introduces faith as the concept opposite to sight; faith to Paul is the confident trust in God's unseen power. Paul writes in Hebrews 11:1, "Now faith is the substance of things hoped for, the evidence of things not seen." We as believers are always saying that we have faith in God, but do we really? In the area of finances and economics many of us are not showing God that we have faith and in some of our cases we are flat out disobedient. Here's what I mean. In the area of insurance, a product in which we cannot see or immediately benefit from, we are not adequately covered to protect our assets and the well-being of our families. Is this faith? I think not. In addition, God has told us in Proverbs 13:22, "A good man leaveth an inheritance to his children's children." God not only instructs us to leave an inheritance but he also gives us the vehicle to use: LIFE INSURANCE. We will talk more about life insurance a bit later.

When it comes to spiritual laws, the multiplication of our finances, we know. is critical in the kingdom of God. We all are familiar with the parable of the talents (money) in which the lord gave three men talents according to their abilities; Jesus continues to say that the lord went away on a long journey and the one servant who was given five talents doubled his; the servant who was given two talents doubled his and the servant who was given one talent hid his. When the lord returned, each man had to give an account of what they had done with what the lord had given them. The lord commended the two servants who increased what the lord had given them. The third servant buried and hid his and gave an excuse just like many believers. However, Jesus indicates that the lord took the only talent that was given to the third servant and gave it to the servant with five talents who increased his to 10. Then Jesus says in Matthew 25:30: "And cast ye the unprofitable servant into outer darkness: there shall be weeping and gnashing of teeth." The unprofitable servant was cast out or excluded from the kingdom. He shared the same fate as a wicked man. He did not fail because he did not invest the money, but rather because his lack of good works showed he lacked saving faith. This is a very serious scripture because it describes HELL. We as believers must understand this spiritual law because it is critically important. I'm not saying that we are to pursue riches nor is Jesus implying the same. However, Jesus is comparing the kingdom of heaven with profitability in what he has graciously given to us. We all will have to give an account of our stewardship while trying to master the human experience.

The parable of the talents also involves another critical aspect of mastering our faith that is: WORKS. James 2:17-20 says, "Even so faith, if it hath not works, is dead being alone. Yea, a man may say, Thou hast faith, and I have works: shew me thy faith without thy works , and I will shew thee my faith by my works. Thou believest that there is one God, thou doest well: the devils also believe, and tremble. But wilt thou know, O vain man, that faith without works is dead?" Believers, how can we say that we have faith without the works to justify our faith? James says of Abraham in James 2:21, "Was not Abraham our father justified by works, when he had offered Isaac his son upon the altar?" James 2: 25 continues, "Likewise also was not Rahab the harlot justified by works, when she had received the messengers, and had sent them out another way?" We must rid ourselves of old church traditions telling us to continue to pray for the electric bill and the mortgage to be paid. God wants us to THINK concerning our financial situation and make decisions according to His word, our faith and works.

Concerning the law of multiplication of money, if the two profitable servants did not go out into the marketplace would they have been able to multiply the talents? I think not. Jesus, when telling this parable, did not mention the word prayer at all. As a matter of fact, there is no mention of anything spiritual. What does that say to you and me? Remember the scripture says, in Ecclesiastes 10:19, "money answers all things." This was written by the richest man who ever lived, Solomon. Jesus also points out when asked to pay taxes in Matthew 22:21, "Render therefore unto Caesar the things which are Caesar's; and unto God the things that are God's." What Christ is saying is that we have a natural responsibility on earth financially to the government and our creditors. We must therefore show God that we have faith in Him by utilizing the economic system that he has ordained in the earth; then and only then is our faith justified by our WORKS. Remember, Hebrews 11:6 says, "Without faith it is impossible to please God." So it stands to reason that no amount of works can compensate for lack of faith. However, we encourage you to put your works behind your faith because God is covenant keeping and He will reward those who diligently seek him.

STEWARDSHIP

Are you anxious to get out of your mediocre worship and into something more important for the Lord? Paul revealed a mystery regarding stewardship in I Corinthians 4:2 when he says, "Moreover it is required in stewards that one be found faithful." Stewards are those in which something has been entrusted and they are responsible and accountable for that they have been given. Each one of us has been entrusted with special and specific gifts from God—a household, children, a career, work in the church, money, all of which makes us all stewards. According to the word of the Lord, stewards are required to be faithful and trustworthy. Ask yourselves a question: how can being a steward determine whether or not God can trust us with bigger things? Our track record, of course; Luke 16:10 says, "He who is faithful in what is least is faithful also in much." We demonstrate our faithfulness and trustworthiness by what we have done with that God has given us in the past. Also, we are called stewards because God has entrusted us with the innermost mystery of His kingdom which is the Gospel message of Jesus Christ. This is the responsibility for which all believers are held accountable.

Remember saints, it took the children of Israel forty years to enter into the promised land, a journey that should have taken only eleven days. It stands to reason that our disobedience coupled with our stiff-necked attitudes regarding our finances will prolong the blessings that God has in store for us. In addition, the Lord will not allow some of us to reach the promises of God because of our attitudes, like the Hebrews in Exodus, where the current generation of Moses was not allowed to enter into the promise of the Lord. DON'T LET THAT BE YOU AND YOUR FAMILY.

SHEEP VS. GOATS

The Bible tells us that the **love** of money is the root of all evil. We as believers have to be careful that we do not allow ourselves to serve mammon (money). Jesus says in Matthew 6:24, "No man can serve two masters: for either he will hate the one, and love the other; or else he will hold to the one, and despise the other. Ye cannot serve God and mammon [money]."

The word "mammon" means "riches" in Aramaic, the language spoken by Jesus and most of the common people of Judea in his day. When we look at **GOD and mammon** they present rival claims and man must make a choice. We as believers must put God first and reject materialism in our lives or we can live for the temporal material things and refuse God's claim on our lives. I know at this point you are thinking what does this have to do with sheep and goats? What does this have to do with economics and money? Everything.

Let's examine one distinguishing characteristic of the goat, an animal that God created. The goat will only follow a person who dangles something in its face. In other words goats will only follow if enticed with something it can eat. If we further study this character in a spiritual content we understand the temptation of Jesus to be one of economical importance and significance. In Matthew 4:8-9, "the devil taketh him up into an exceeding high mountain, and sheweth him all the kingdoms of the world and the glory of them; And saith unto him, All these things will I give thee, if thou wilt fall down and worship me." The word temptation means simply to entice as used in the King James

Version of the bible. However, its primary meaning is to "prove" or "test." This third temptation involved the lust of the eyes where it is significant to understand that Satan tried to use the wealth and materialism of this world to tempt our Lord. We as believers must understand that Satan does the same with us regarding the wealth and splendor of this world; he will attempt to lure us with the big house, car, clothing and the relentless pursuit of money, all of which can easily become an idol if we are not careful. Ask yourselves a question: what is the world dangling in my face? Am I a goat? Aren't we all blessed that Jesus was not a goat herder but a shepherd? Yes we are. The simple fact that Jesus resisted this material temptation indicates to you and I that we can also resist this temptation because of our faith in the Lord who has conquered the lust of the eyes.

Matthew 25:41–45 describes the goats as unrighteous and told to "depart from Him into the everlasting fire prepared for the devil and his angels"; they were told this because they failed to care for Him during the terrible times and neglected His followers, which constituted neglect of Himself. This neglect the Bible speaks of is the opposite of what the sheep did: the goats did not feed Him or His followers, did not give Him or them water, did not clothe Him or them, did not accept Him when He was a stranger, and did not visit when He or they were sick or imprisoned. Let's look deeper into the goats' neglect of Christ' followers; it all involves economic implications, that is, food, water, clothing and transportation to go to the hospital or prison. Again when we look at the characteristic of a goat we see a very selfish ambition to only follow that which will satisfy the goats' worldly (fleshly) desires. Be careful saints; do not be enticed by pastors who always dangle a pot of gold every Sunday in the pulpit in which their mere motivational speeches encourage you to hold onto a word from week to week without education, application and implementation.

SHEEP

In Matthew 25:33-40 the king places the sheep on His right hand, but the goats on the left. He then invites the sheep to enter His glorious kingdom, prepared for them from the foundation of the world. Unlike the goats, the sheep fed Him when He was hungry, gave Him drink when thirsty, welcomed Him when He was a stranger, clothed Him when ill-clad and visited Him in sickness and in prison. The Lord also created the sheep and gave distinguishing character traits unique to them. One of the more spiritual connotative traits are the fact that sheep will follow anyone at anytime **without being enticed by anything.** This is why pastors and ministers are held accountable for the leadership of God's people.

The fact that sheep are very peaceful, nonaggressive, conforming animals that are willing to follow at all cost God calls the followers of Jesus sheep. Jesus, is called the Lamb of God in John 1: 29; also Jesus is referred to as the Good Shepherd in Isaiah 40: 11, "He shall feed His flock like a shepherd: He shall gather the lambs with His arm, and carry them in His bosom, and shall gently lead those that are with young." The Lord fully understands that every sheep needs a shepherd's guidance, protection and nurturing for mature growth and development. Sheep do not need to be enticed or have material wealth dangled in their faces to follow Jesus.. They follow God's word because of their faith and belief. A very important check for pastors and ministers: are your sermons creating sheep or goats? Are your churches well attended because of the word or because you are a good motivational speaker? Sheep follow Christ and God's word, whereas goats follow pastors and ministers.

ECONOMIC PLAGUES

THE TALE OF TWO ECONOMIES

From 2000–2003 we have seen a bearish or down economy because of the sovereign hand of a mighty God. Don't think that God is in the midst of only this economy; let's examine Egypt during the time of the Hebrew captivity.

For 400 years we see God's people helping to economically build and financially empower an ungodly nation. Remember, in Ecclesiastes, chapter 3, the Bible talks about everything having its time or season; it was the time and season for God to keep the covenant that He promised to Abraham. The infinite attribute of God is expressed as **Omnipotence, Omniscience and Omnipresence**. God's omnipotence means that He is able to do all which is consistent with His nature and will. His omniscience means He knows all things instantaneously and eternally. Omnipresence means He is present in all points of space and time. Therefore, God fully understands what is at the center of the civilization of man: **HIS ECONOMIC STRUCTURE.** Let us take a look at God's hand in the Egyptian economy. When God wants to attain glory in the earth He blesses a people on one hand and he curses a people on the other. In His word, Deuteronomy chapter 30:19 God says, "I call heaven and earth as witnesses today against you, that I have set before you life and death, blessing and cursing; therefore choose life, that both you and your descendants may live." In addition, we see that descendants (future generations of a family) may live based on the **choices we make** (spiritually as well as financially).

God's curses came in the form of plagues on an ungodly nation. God's intent, we can so vividly see, was designed to destroy the economic structure of this ungodly society. When we hear the word plague what does it mean? It means any afflictive evil, scourge or infestation. God used it as an outpouring of pestilence to punish the Egyptians for not allowing the Hebrews to leave Egypt. These ten plagues included: turning of water to blood, the plague of frogs, lice, flies, murrain on the cattle of the land, boils, locusts, darkness and death of the firstborn. These plagues all brought economic commerce to a complete standstill.

In our economy today, we see signs of plagues that are unique in our society: unemployment at 6.4%; consumer expectation numbers low; manufacturing orders down; supply outweighing demand; national debt growing and soon expected to reach an all-time high in several years, estimated at $455 billion dollars (causing future generations of our children to pay a higher tax rate); fraudulent accounting practices and CEOs lying and stealing. In addition, September 11th changed the world both spiritually and financially. Spiritually, there was a national prayer day implemented by the President and thus an outpouring of God's spirit in the land. Financially, fear grasped the hearts of man sending the financial markets downward and catapulting the American economy into a recession from which we are still recovering.

Keep in mind that God is still in control and has ordained this economy for such a time. We as the body of believers have to educate ourselves and know what to do in the midst of a famine. Now that we see God's sovereign hand in our economy, let's begin to educate ourselves for the journey that lies ahead.

CHAPTER 2
PROGRAMMING

Programming is the single most critical aspect in determining our financial destiny in the earth. We are going to examine the internal organs that God has given to us to create and develop within ourselves the attitudes and behaviors that are necessary to propel us into our economic purpose as ambassadors for Christ.

THE WORLD PROGRAMS

For many of us it is very difficult to deprogram and reprogram our attitudes regarding economics because the world has programmed us at a most impressionable time, from birth to eighteen. It is during these years the world teaches us it's cool to be consumers, go into debt and not to worry about paying bills on time. In addition, our public school systems do not teach our children how money works and do not teach our children how interest affects what they buy on credit or the significance of paying bills on time with regard to the impact it has on one's credit report.

A parable: There were two shoe salesmen who stumbled across a lost island in the South Pacific. This island had 1,000,000 inhabitants. What was unique about this island was that nobody was wearing shoes. The one salesman called his company and reported he had stumbled across an island where nobody was wearing shoes; he said to himself, "I cannot make any money here," so he decided to leave the island as fast as he could. The other salesman called his company and said to them, "Sell everything we have and send me a million pairs of shoes; there is a tremendous market here." Which of the two salesmen are you? Remember, life is 10% of what happens to us and 90% of how we react to it.

Before we repented and were converted in the knowledge of Jesus Christ, we were born into sin and shaped in iniquity. Therefore, the world controlled our minds along with our sinful members. The world then took advantage of our youth and educated us in its sinful culture and we began to lay the groundwork for our economic future.

Thanks be to God that He has predetermined our lives and our economic destinies to be effective representatives in the earth for His glory. The struggles between the flesh and the spirit war against each other to control our minds and members. However, the difficult transformation is to renew our minds daily according to God's word and to not conform to this world and its economic culture.

We know that man resembles God in certain ways; just as God is a Trinity (Father, Son and Holy Spirit), so man is a tripartite being (spirit, soul and body). Now we will examine the components of the natural body.

THE LAW OF THE MIND

When we even start to consider the magnificent creation of our minds, it is an infinite thought. Our minds contain eighteen billion cells all ready to be programmed. Our minds can recall 800 images per second. Our minds function in the same manner as the CPU (central processing unit) of a computer. Our minds have what I call a RUME2 (pronounced "are you me too") mechanism designed for self-identification. This is how it works: the RU is the monitor and it brings up all of the images and puts it on a screen in your mind, and the ME2 is the mechanism that reads and identifies what is on the screen. For example, try not to think about an orange; you couldn't help it the minute you saw the word "orange." Your RU put it on the screen and your ME2 read it to be an orange. Believers, here is the beginning of understanding; whatever we continue to do repeatedly with regard to money before we were saved, the RU put the image on the screen daily and the ME2 daily read the same image, therefore causing self-identification principles to take place in our minds.

These self-identification financial principles were first introduced in our minds as behaviors and then became permanent fixtures within the subconscious mind creating worldly attitudes within our hearts regarding money.

It is so important for us as believers to guard the information that we are absorbing on a daily basis. We are to protect our minds from the world and its views regarding finances by the word of the Lord. Romans 12:2 says, "And be not conformed to this world: but be ye transformed by the **renewing of your mind that ye may prove what is that good and acceptable, and perfect will of God." Our minds must be constantly and consistently renewed daily by the word of the Lord.** Remember believers, our goal is to have a spirit-controlled mind to control our fleshly members.

I hear you asking why do we have to renew our minds daily? Romans 8:7 says to us, "Because the carnal mind is enmity against God: for it is not subject to the Law of God, neither indeed can be." After Adam's sin the law of our minds became dominated by our flesh and under its direction and control. Walk in the spirit and you will make financial decisions based on the word of the Lord.

CONSCIOUS VS. SUBCONSCIOUS MIND

This is a very powerful concept that you **must** understand. All you have to do is to associate the conscious mind with behaviors and the subconscious mind with an attitude. This is how it works. Let's say you want to be a millionaire by the time you reach the age of 30. However, you have no financial training or economic understanding. When you put the image of a big house and a yacht on your RU screen the ME2 will read it and the self identification mechanism will say to you, "This is definitely not you." What you have just done is to create a behavior in your mind. For example, how many of you have had New Year's resolutions to lose weight and never get started or get started for one month and quit? You created a behavior in the consciousness of your mind. It did not turn into an attitude because you did not put it on your screen long enough for your ME2 to identify the thought as an attitude. The way you get it to be an attitude is to continually think about what you want by giving it shape, size, color and definition on a daily basis and continue to allow your ME2 to read it. Eventually it will become an attitude because it goes from the conscious mind to the subconscious mind. From the subconscious mind it will go to the final destination, which is your heart, and then it becomes one with you. Remember, the key is to renew your goals daily in your mind by doing things like driving around exclusive neighborhoods with $500,000- to million-dollar homes and visualizing yourself living in the area, if this is your desire. Getting back to our millionaire status it is critically important after you program yourself to have a vehicle (plan) that will take you to your goal or dream. The secret to a successful economic and financial life is to have oneness with mind (RUME2), heart and spirit. Now let's examine the heart and its function in this process.

LAW OF THE HEART

The heart is the central organ of the body and has come to stand for the center of moral, intellectual and spiritual life. The heart is the organ by which God identifies mankind. There are 821 Scripture references using the word "heart." God said in His word in Proverbs 21:2, "Every way of a man is right in his own eyes: but the Lord pondereth the hearts." The heart is most critical in the programming process because God said in his word in Proverbs 23:7, "As a man thinketh in his heart so is he." Remember what we said are the steps in programming:

1. Think about desired goals or objectives (daily)
2. Continue until RUME2 agrees
3. Conscious behavior becomes subconscious attitude.
4. Attitude becomes heart condition
5. Proverbs 23:7: As you think in your hearts so are you.

The Lord knew the significance of the heart of man because in Matthew 22:37 God pointed out man's obligation with the first and great commandment, "You shall love the Lord your God with all your **heart,** with all your soul, and with all your mind." The significance is that the heart is mentioned first. In addition the concept of oneness is being identified with heart, soul and mind. It stands to reason that the heart and mind play an intricate role in the development of programming and oneness within the natural man.

The significance of programming is to eliminate believers from mental bondage.

Many of us have been delivered from physical bondage but we are still enslaved mentally when it comes to our current economic attitudes. It stands to reason that when we have repented and been converted into the faith, we experience a transformation as an individual and all things become new. We must understand that in addition to the change of our heart condition, we must also experience the same transformation with the renewing of our minds economically and financially. Our old way of economics used when we were in the world does not apply in the kingdom of God.

POWER OF LIFE & DEATH

Many of us as believers speak death to our economic prosperity because of how we were programmed in the world through our experiences and circumstances. Proverbs 18:21 clearly says to us," Death and Life are in the power of the tongue." We as believers are very familiar with this passage of scripture yet we say things like, "I'm broke" or "We don't have any money" or "We'll never be able to afford that" or "We'll never have a lifestyle like that." The point is God's word says that he has no respected persons and through Christ Jesus **ALL** things are possible to them that believe. So, what's the problem? God gave us the answer in Ezekiel 37:1–10, the Valley of the Dry Bones. God is asking us the question, can you financially prosper? The Lord is saying to us as he said to Ezekiel, prophesy to your financial situation and speak words of life to your current economic condition. Prophesy to your finances a desirable future state or condition you would like to be in because God's word says, "To call those things that be not as though they were." After you have prophesied to your financial condition add faith coupled with works and in due season what you have sown you will reap.

Saints, I want to illustrate to you what happens in the spirit realm regarding the role of Satan and how he uses our negative words to impact our financial lives and destinies. In Job 1: 6–7 the word of the Lord says," Now there was a day when the sons of God (angels)came to present themselves before the Lord, **and Satan (in Hebrew means accuser) came also among them.**" And the Lord said to Satan, whence comest thou? Then Satan answered the Lord and said "From going to and fro in the earth, and walking up and down in it." We know the rest of this story: God boasted about the uprightness of His servant Job and Satan told the Lord that the only reason Job was walking upright before Him is because He (God) had a hedge of protection around him.

Let's examine this closely because we see Satan the accuser walking to and fro up and down the earth searching for God's righteous people to accuse them of only showing obedience and loyalty because of God's protective hands around our lives. If we understand how the accuser works, then we should understand when we use negative words to describe our financial condition that the accuser stands before God and emphasizes to Him what we said. Then the Lord, being holy, has to do what His word says. If we speak death to our economic condition Satan goes before the throne and accuses us; God must honor His word, and we will suffer financially because of our negative words.

COMFORTABLE VS. UNCOMFORTABLE

When it comes to finances and economics, being comfortable or uncomfortable plays a major role in the plan of God for the utilization of the believer in the world. The believer who feels that he/she is very comfortable economically may not realize the full covenant benefits of the kingdom. Why, you ask? Because God throughout the Bible has used men and women and made them uncomfortable while using them for His purpose. The world promotes comfort and a mediocre standard of living. This is evident by the study done in 1955 in the financial services industry. They followed 100 men over the course of their lives and found that by the age of sixty-five that ninety-one were dead or dead broke; five were wealthy and four were rich. Do you think that being comfortable led to the ninety-one either dying or being poor in retirement? I'm sure it contributed tremendously to the outcome. As we will see in the upcoming chapters, financial planning plays a vital role in our retirement future.

Do you think you are reaching your full potential in God by living from paycheck to paycheck? Being indebted? Not being able to tithe 10% of your gross income? Working for someone else for a living? If your answer to any of these questions are yes, then you are comfortable and are accepting your circumstances as they are. You are not experiencing the full benefits of the kingdom of a loving God and Father.

Being comfortable says that you do not need to educate yourself about money and the economy; being comfortable promotes the spirit of consumerism (spending); in addition, comfort keeps us from being a good credit risk by keeping us not informed. If you are truly comfortable in your finances and economics make sure you have mastered the following categories:

1. Know the rule of 72 (how money works)
2. D.I.M.E. theory of insurance (be properly covered)

3. Disability insurance coverage

4. Emergency fund (6–12 months' cash reserves)

5. College funding for children

6. Retirement planning

7. Estate planning

8. Long-term care planning

The law of comfort says if you continue to do the same thing year after year you will receive the same results. On the other hand, if you continue to do the same thing year after year and expect different results then you are **INSANE.**

If you are uncomfortable in your financial situation, please don't be alarmed. The Lord has placed within you a desire to improve your current economic status. Remember, the Lord used men and women in the Bible for His purpose but he first made them very uncomfortable in their current life situations. When you are not comfortable, you have purpose in your heart to reach a degree of comfort through action. The key here is to do something you have never done in order to have something you have never had.

If you have not satisfied all of these areas of planning and you consider your financial situation comfortable you must THINK AGAIN. There is no security in this world's financial system, as millions are unemployed. We will discuss in greater detail all of these areas of planning in the coming chapters of this book.

UNCOMFORTALBE

God in His infinite wisdom used many people in the Bible, and they were all made to be uncomfortable for His purpose and will. The degree of their discomfort only increased their effectiveness in the situation in which they were used. Do you think that Abraham, Joseph, Moses, David, Joshua, the disciples and Jesus himself were uncomfortable in their missions and purposes in God? I'm sure they were. If comfort promoted financial security and economic understanding, then a higher percentage of people would be financially independent and self-employed. Discomfort gives us a burning desire to become more in God's kingdom and a broader understanding of our full potential in Christ both spiritually and naturally. Discomfort says to us that we must put our faith in God and not our own abilities. In addition, we will have confidence in the realm of the unseen and according to Jesus in John 20:29, "blessed are those who have not seen and yet believe."

In terms of economic and financial planning it is far better to be uncomfortable now and very comfortable later than being comfortable now and very uncomfortable later. We as believers should not be conformed to this world according to Romans 12:2. The word world used here means the society or system that man has built in order to make himself happy without God. Remember, the god and prince of this world is Satan (2 Cor.4:4 and John 12:31, 14:30 and 16:11). Satan seeks to attract through the lust of the flesh, the eyes and the pride of life. The world has its own lifestyles, thought patterns, money views and religion. The world seeks to get everyone to conform to its culture and customs. Whatever the world says about money and economics is completely contrary to what we should do as believers. If the world promotes comfort, being average and mediocre in your finances, then we as believers should do the opposite of the world and what it says. Your mindset should be one of going against your cousins, uncles, brothers and sisters if they are conformed to this world and be the example for Christ on the earth. Remember saints, if you are willing to do what others are not, you are saying to God that you want to be more than a mediocre Christian.

My personal wake-up call came when I became sick and tired of nothing ever working (when I was conformed to the world). Because it was not working the many years I did it my way, I decided to do it God's way by "**first seeking the kingdom of God and His righteousness and all these things will be added to you.**"

Let me tell that the Lord's way is working very well and I now know that it truly is God (and not the world) who gives us the power to get wealth.

PROSPERITY
(RIGHTEOUS)

Have you ever thought to yourself, "Does God want me to be prosperous?" Why do the unsaved have so much wealth and possessions and the believers struggle?

Consider God's word in Psalms 36:8, "They shall be abundantly satisfied with the fatness of thy house; and thou shalt make them drink of the river of thy pleasures." In Psalms 37:11, it is said "But the meek shall inherit the earth; and shall delight themselves in the abundance of peace." Psalms 37:18: "The Lord knoweth the days of the upright: and their inheritance shall be forever." Psalms 37:19: "They shall not be ashamed in the evil time; and in the days of **famine** they shall be satisfied." Psalms 84:11: "For the Lord God is a sun and shield: the Lord will give grace and glory; no good thing will he withhold from them that walk uprightly." Psalms 92:12: "The righteous shall flourish like the palm tree; he shall grow like a cedar in Lebanon."

PROSPERITY

(WICKED)

What does the Lord say about the wicked who prosper? Job 21:13: "They spend their days in wealth, and in a moment go down to the grave." Psalms 73:5: "They are not in trouble as other men; neither are they plagued like other men." Psalms 73:6: "Therefore pride compasseth them about as a chain; violence covereth them about as a garment." Psalms 73:7: "Their eyes stand out with fatness: they have more than heart could wish." Psalms 73:12:"Behold, these are the ungodly, who prosper in the world; they increase in riches." Why do the wicked prosper on Earth, you ask? They understand the following spiritual and natural laws on Earth:

1. Seed time and harvest time (sowing and reaping)
2. Giving 10% of their money to needy causes (multiplication of money)
3. Sacrifice and discipline
4. Oneness within themselves regarding purpose and mission
5. Understanding debt and credit
6. Understanding economics
7. Understanding financial markets
8. Understand that change is inevitable
9. **Reading, reading, reading**
10. Watching financial television (CNN, MSNBC, CNBC, Bloomberg television)

When we see the ungodly prosper we need to keep in mind that God's word tells us that the wealth of the wicked is laid up for the righteous. We see God's word being manifested in the Old Testament when the Hebrews took possession of the promised land from the wicked by force. There are natural laws on Earth that will allow this transference to manifest itself, but we have to educate and prepare ourselves for the transformation. We will discuss later the natural laws in place right now that will allow this wealth transfer.

UNITY & ONENESS

LAW OF SPIRITUAL & NATURAL MANIFESTATION

(Internal and External)

The Lord God in His infinite wisdom has orchestrated within us the gift of natural manifestation. The mystery in tapping into this gift is found in the Triune nature of God. Jesus reveals God's nature when He gives the disciples the Great Commission in Matthew 28:19, "Go ye therefore, and teach all nations, baptizing them in the name of the Father, and of the Son, and of the Holy Ghost." We see the significance of unity and oneness in the Godhead and in the body. In Ephesians 4:4–6, Paul says, "There is one body, and one Spirit, even as ye are called in one hope of your calling; One Lord, one faith, one baptism, One God and Father of all, who is above all, and through all, and in you all."

In addition to God's Triune nature He created man as a tripartite being (spirit, soul and body). God gave man components in his natural body that through unity and oneness in purpose and mission natural manifestation could be achieved. To further illustrate this point let's look at the Great Commandment. In Matthew 22:37, Jesus summarizes man's obligation to God by saying, "You shall love the Lord your God with all your **heart,** with all your **soul,** and with all your **mind.**" I purposely put in bold print the three components of natural manifestation within mankind. God created us in His own likeness and image so he is very familiar with His creation. Therefore, he gives us instructions to accomplish the love he desires by giving us the blueprint of natural manifestation: unity and oneness of purpose and mission. This point can be completely understood when Jesus said in Mark 3:25, "And if a house be divided against itself, that house cannot stand." This is the internal law of natural manifestation. There is another law of natural manifestation and it is external.

The laws of external natural manifestation can be found in Habakkuk 2:2–3, "Write the vision, and make it plain upon tables that he may run that reads it. For the vision is yet for an appointed time, but at the end it shall speak, and not lie: though it tarry, wait for it; because it will surely come, it will not tarry." In addition to giving us the blueprint for natural manifestation God gave us an example of this scripture: The Old Testament tells of the coming of Christ. It is God's way of writing His vision; Jesus himself reads the vision and runs with it or works it (the vision); Christ' crucifixion and resurrection are the result of the vision speaking or manifesting itself. If we consider our financial situation we then must **write our plans on paper, run with our plan or work it, and according to God's word the vision will speak or naturally manifest itself.** The vision may tarry but we are encouraged to wait for it because God has promised us it will surely come.

The Laws of Spiritual Manifestation can be found in Romans 10: 9–10, "that if thou shall confess with thy mouth the Lord Jesus, and shall believe in thine heart that God has raised him from the dead, thou shall be saved. For with the heart man believes unto righteousness; and with the mouth confession is made unto salvation." We see that the key words in the above mentioned scripture are **confess and mouth, heart and believe. God reveals to us how we can achieve salvation from a spiritual point of view.** We as believers can incorporate this law in our finances. How, you ask? Simply apply the law, believe in your heart and confess with your mouth that you will be debt-free.

This is what we need to do to experience the fullness or completeness of God financially:

1. Confess with our mouths debt freedom and financial prosperity.
2. Believe in our hearts in debt freedom and financial prosperity
3. Write down our plans of debt freedom and financial prosperity.
4. Work our debt-free and financial prosperity plans. Then:
5. Debt freedom and financial prosperity is achieved or manifested.

SOWING & REAPING

Galatians 6:7–8 says," Be not deceived, God is not mocked: for whatsoever a man soweth, that shall he reap. For he that soweth of the flesh shall reap corruption; but he that soweth to the Spirit shall of the Spirit reap life everlasting." What does this mean? How does this have anything to do with finances? Let's look at this passage in laymen's terms. If a farmer sows wheat his harvest is wheat. When the farmer sows wheat, there are several factors that will determine the harvest: the type of ground he is sowing in, the soil, moisture, sunlight, and most important, the season. We see that we reap in greater quantities than what we sow, sometimes thirtyfold, sixtyfold and sometimes a hundredfold.

How do we effectively apply this spiritual law to our finances? Well, let's look at what the scripture says. When we talk about sowing to the flesh we are talking about buying that pair of $100 shoes with the money marked for paying the light bill; we are talking about buying name-brand clothing, purchasing household goods on credit, and going to the mall every weekend just to look. Saints, if you sow spending you will reap indebtedness. If you sow watching BET rap videos for three hours you will reap entertainment. If you sow not paying your bills on time you will reap a disaster for a credit score. If you sow being uneducated you will reap ignorance. All of the sowing after the flesh will reap corruption in harvest. Each of the examples will cause stressful financial circumstances in our lives. What happens next will further complicate matters economically because the circumstances then forces us to make an ungodly decision regarding our finances. We then go deeper into debt, our credit report is a mess and we have more month than money. At this point for many of us the only answer is bankruptcy. (Do not declare bankruptcy; we are children of the most high God and this should not be an option for us.)

What we should sow is study of God's word because we shall reap life everlasting. We need to sow study of economics and money we shall reap knowledge and understanding. We need to sow study of the laws of supply and demand; we need to sow how to manage and multiply money. We need to sow learning how the economy works and how it affects us. We should not sow to our flesh because it is our earthly desires and it says to God that we want to spend our money on ourselves for our pleasures and comforts. However, if we sow to the Spirit we are telling God that we will use our money for the furtherance of His interest. Financial development is critical because there are people out there who God has determined only we can minister to because of our circumstances. Come on, people are waiting to hear the gospel of Christ and the Lord has chosen you to bring them into His family. Those people are depending on you.

What is equally important for us as believers to understand is when we sow to the things of the Spirit we need not be anxious because Paul reminds us in Galatians 6:9 that the rewards are very certain, even if they are not immediate. Remember, you do not sow wheat today and receive the harvest tomorrow. The significant point I want to make is keep sowing that Spiritual seed faithfully and you will see the rewards in the Spiritual realm in due season.

CHAPTER 3

THE STORY OF MONEY

Thomas Jefferson once said, "If the American people allow the bankers to control the issue of money, first by inflation and then by deflation, the bankers and corporations will deprive the people of their property until their children will wake up homeless on the continent their fathers conquered."

We live in the richest nation on earth and always seem to run out of money. Women are working just to help make ends meet, men are working overtime and part time and children are working little jobs to help out. Still, our debt climbs higher and psychologists say that many divorces are the product of the lack of money.

Let's look at money and its creation. Money is very inexpensive to make and the people who create the money will make a tremendous profit. Consider this: grocers make 2% to 5% profit, car makers sell their cars for only a 1% to 2% profit above manufacturers cost and that is considered good business practices; however, money manufacturers have no limit on their profits. It costs the same to make a $1 bill as it does to make a $10,000 bill. Let's look at this love of money which the Bible calls the "root of all evil."

First of all, we need an adequate supply of money to be able to function in our civilized society. Without money, industry would stop, food would disappear, jobs would not be created, farms would cease to exist, government would cease to exist and we would have a system of anarchy in place; civilized human beings would become violent just to survive. If we remove money or reduce the adequate supply of money, we have the Great Depression of the 1930s.

Consider the Great Depression of the 1930s. America possessed fertile farm land, skilled workers, industrial capacity, road networks, communication devices, railroad systems, waterways and an efficient government structure. Why was there a depression and who was responsible? Remember what Thomas Jefferson said about giving the money control to the bankers? Well, because of the lack of money in circulation we experienced the worst financial crisis in American history. Why are we talking about this, you ask? Because I want the body of Christ to fully understand how money works in America. The bankers just stopped lending money to industry, farmers and retailers. However, payments on previous loans had to be made as money disappeared from circulation. Here lies the fatality of it all; the bankers then foreclosed on stores, farms and industries and the people were told that times were hard and there was no money. The people were robbed of their possessions and livelihood.

Then after the end of World War II, the same bankers who had no money to lend in the 1930s had billions of dollars to lend in the 1940s—go figure. The nation did not have food for sale in 1934 but could now finance bombs, planes, uniforms and ships to finance the war. How ironic is that? No money in peacetime but billions of dollars in wartime.

MONEY REGULATION

Our founding fathers recognized the power of money in a civilized society and delegated the responsibility to coin and print money to the federal government. They wrote in simple English and I quote, "Congress shall have the Power to Coin Money and Regulate the Value Thereof."

The bad news is that in 1913, Congress passed the Federal Reserve Act that authorized the establishment of the Federal Reserve Corporation, with a Federal Board of Directors to run the Corporation and they divided the United states into 12 Federal Reserve Districts. (I'm not criticizing the system, just giving the facts.) When this piece of legislation passed, the control of money disappeared from Congress and reappeared in the hands of the Federal Reserve Corporation and Board (bankers).

Let's look at how our monetary system works. We know that our government spends more than it takes in with taxes; let's say the government needs $87 billion dollars to rebuild Iraq (which the president is proposing). Understand, saints of God, that our government does not have the money so it (the government) must go to the creators of money for the $87 billion. (Remember the government no longer has the power to coin and regulate money.) Do you think that that the Federal Reserve Bank gives the government free money? Of course not. The bankers give the government $87 billion based on the government's agreement to pay it back with **INTEREST.** Congress then authorizes the Treasury Department to print the $87 billion in U.S. Bonds, which is then delivered to the Federal Reserve Bank. The Federal Reserve Bank then pays the cost of printing ($1,000) and then makes the exchange. The government will then pay its obligations. Saints, at this point we the people are indebted without the possibility of ever paying for this transaction because we would only be paying billions of dollars in interest without ever paying any principal. Consider this, in the 1980s the government was over 1 trillion dollars in debt; we paid in excess of 100 billion dollars in interest alone.

Believers, I want you to understand this important concept; if you borrow $60,000 you must pay back $255,931 at a 14% interest rate for 30 years. You must agree to pay $710.92 per month, totaling $255,931.92.Consider this, when you borrow $60,000 you are putting $60,000 into circulation. The interest paid is not created, therefore it is not added to money in circulation. So you are taking the $255,931.92 out of circulation by paying almost $200,000 more in interest. The point is that debtors can never pay off lenders because as they pay principal and interest the money supply is constantly being reduced.

Saints, it is vitally important for God's people to get out and stay out of debt. Just because the world promotes indebtedness, that alone should remind us to be separate from the world, as the Bible tells us. In addition Proverbs 22:7 says, "**THE BORROWER IS A SLAVE TO THE LENDER.**" Debt is a form of bondage that enslaves mankind because it requires an exorbitant amount of interest. Debt limits man's ability to take advantage of ministerial opportunities.

MASTERING THE GAME OF MONEY

Do you know how to win the money game? Do you know how to multiply money? If your answer is no, join the 90% club of people who have not been exposed to the rule of 72. What is the rule of 72 you ask? It is simply dividing 72 by the interest rate to estimate how long it takes your money to double. Mr. Albert Einstein called compound interest the eighth wonder of the world. Let's illustrate:

Age	2% Money doubles 36 yrs		6% money doubles 12 yrs		12% money doubles 6 yrs
25	$5,000	25	$5,000	25	$5,000
61	$10,000	37	$10,000	31	$10,000
		49	$20,000	37	$20,000
		61	$40,000	43	$40,000
				49	$80,000
				55	$160,000
				61	$320,000

Let's analyze the chart because this is the most important point I want you to understand. Let's look at 2% where our money doubles every 36 years (72/2 = 36). Believers, if you are putting money in a bank for retirement please **STOP IT TODAY. Banks will take your money, invest it in mutual funds and receive a double-digit return, and give you only 2% and a toaster.** Please understand that if you are 25 with $5,000 your money will not double until you are age 61. (Money doubles 1 time before retirement.) You will only have $10,000 for retirement. Let's look at 6%: your money doubles every 12 years (72/6 = 12). If you are 25 with $5,000 your money will double only 3 times before retirement. You will only retire with $40,000. How long will that last? Now, let's look at 12%, where your money will double every 6 years (72/12 = 6). At 12% your money doubles 6 times in 36 years. Which of the totals at 61 would you want to have, $10,000, $40,000 or $320,000? Saints, eliminate the middleman in your retirement planning strategies. Who is the middleman, you ask? **It is the bank.**

INFLATION & DEFLATION

As a believer it is critically important to understand that our economy is cyclical, to know the economic indicators and understand what to do when that particular economic condition is present.

INFLATION

Inflation is unique in nature because it causes most of us to have a spirit of consumerism. What I mean is it forces us into a buy-right-now mentality. What actually happens is we are very motivated to buy because we feel that prices are about to climb. Think of inflation this way: picture blowing air into a balloon and it expanding. The expansion represents money being put into the economy. Remember we talked about the Federal Reserve Bank having control over the monetary system; this is what happens: The Federal Reserve Banks have many member banks and those member banks have to pay reserves to the Federal Bank. Inflation is caused by the Federal Bank lowering its reserve amounts that the member banks have to pay to the Federal bank. This gives the banks more cash money to loan to businesses and consumers. This puts money in circulation because businesses as well as consumers refinance debt. Businesses and consumers spend more for goods and services; this causes demand to outweigh supply and forces prices to increase. Businesses hire more employees to provide goods and services to keep pace with demand. Manufacturers have to keep pace with orders to make money, so they too hire more employees and expand payroll to meet demand. This causes prices of materials to increase, and with expanded payrolls overall costs are increased. What happens next is an increase in prices because of an increase in overall costs. What this does is to decrease the purchasing power of our dollar. Keep in mind in 1954 $1 was worth a dollar in purchasing power. In 1993 $1 was worth .16. To illustrate this point even more, in 1979 the cost of a pay phone call was .10; today it is .50. The average price of a new car was $6,800; today it is $20,600. The average cost of a new home was $80,000; today it is $180,000. The cost of a stamp was .10; today it is .37. This is why, saints of God, we must get out of debt and multiply money for the sake of our children.

The mechanics of inflation are low interest rates, less stringent credit criteria, low unemployment, increased government and business spending and increased consumer spending. The key in this type of economy is to get out of debt and increase your cash reserves. We will now see why it is important for us to build our cash reserves when we talk about deflation. Remember, the world and the bankers promote spending during inflationary periods, but this causes us to suffer tremendous economic hardships in the deflationary period.

DEFLATION

Deflation is caused by just the opposite of inflation. The Federal Reserve Bank increases the minimum reserves it requires from the member banks. This causes the banks to keep more money in reserves and have less money to loan to businesses and consumers. This reduces the amount of money in circulation and cash becomes tight. Businesses begin to lay off the excess amount of employees they hired during the inflationary period. (This is why an emergency fund is critical, and also why you should not spend during the inflationary period.) Consumers begin to spend less for goods and services and prices begin to fall. It is during this economic cycle that many people who refinanced their homes get laid off and face foreclosure (we will discuss later how those with cash can get wealthy during this period). It is during this cycle that interest rates will increase and credit criteria become very stringent. This biggest advantage for having cash during this cycle is the foreclosure market. There are over one million foreclosures in this country. If we are cash-ready we can buy real estate for pennies on the dollar.

The mechanics of deflation are: high unemployment rate, high interest rates, prices becoming too high for consumers to make purchases, consumers spending less, government and businesses spending less, money becoming tight in the economy and credit criteria becoming more stringent. Saints, it is critically important for us to know the signs and understand what to do in order to protect our families from economic meltdowns.

CHAPTER 4

CREDIT

Your credit report is the single most important file in your financial life. It is an indication of how you manage your finances. The Bible says in Proverbs 22:1," A good name is to be chosen rather than great riches, loving favor rather than silver and gold." Remember saints, your credit file says many things about you as an individual. What does your credit file say about your name? Does your credit file represent Christ? If the answer is no, this section will be of tremendous benefit to you. First let's review the Consumer Credit Bill of Rights:

1. The right to know what is in your credit file and to receive a written copy of that report for a stated fee and with proper identification.

2. The right to receive a free credit report within thirty days (per the Fair Credit Reporting Act) of being denied credit or employment based on information in a credit report.

3. The right to request verification of information in the file and to have it removed if inaccurate or unverifiable information, and to have those results sent to anyone who has received your credit report within the past six months or two years (if for employment) if you so request.

4. The right to know who has received your credit report within the past six months, or in the last two years if received for employment purposes.

5. The right to add a statement of 100 words or less to your credit file to explain any disputed information.

6. The right to have your credit report only accessible to those entities with a permissible purpose.

7. The right to have adverse information purged after seven years (or the time period set by law) from the date of last activity (including successfully completed Chapter 13 bankruptcy) or after ten years (or per your state's legislation) for unsuccessfully completed Chapter 7, 11, 12, 13 bankruptcies or any filings or dismissal of any bankruptcies.

8. The right to have your name and address removed from any direct marketing solicitation which uses data from a credit reporting company.

Now that we understand our rights as consumers, let's develop a plan of attack to re-establish our credit file to represent Christ on the Earth.

CREDIT cont'd

Let's consider the steps to eliminate negative reporting in our file and restore our good name.

1. **Order your credit report.**

2. **Go over the report looking for inaccuracies or already settled debts.**

3. **Write letters to credit bureau with proof of inaccuracies and disputed debts (100 words or less).**

4. **Check credit report twice a year.**

5. **If report is accurate, go back to debt section and negotiate debt to eliminate it.**

The following addresses are for the main three credit reporting agencies:

1. **Experian**

   P.O. Box 9595

   Allen, TX 75013

   (800) 422-4879

2. **Trans Union**

   P.O. Box 2000

   Chester, PA 19022

   (800) 916-8800

3. **Equifax**

   P.O. Box 74021

   Atlanta, GA 30374-0241

   (800) 685-1111

It is recommended to request your credit report by mail.

In order to request a copy of your credit report, you must provide your full name, address, Social Security number and birth date. The agencies will also require two forms of ID (copy of driver's license or state I.D., copy of Social Security card and bill with current address). You can receive a free copy of your file if you send information on the company that denied you credit within the past 60 days; otherwise the normal fee is $8.00 in the form of a check or money order.

REQUEST FOR CREDIT REPORT
(SAMPLE FORM)

Full Name _____

Present Address _____

_____

Social Security Number _____

Date of Birth _____

Signature _____

Date _____

_____ I was denied credit within the past 60 days   _____

          company name

_____ I was denied employment because of adverse credit information   _____

          company name

_____ I was denied insurance or rental property because of adverse credit information

          _____

          company name

_____ I understand that this report will be sent at no charge.

_____ Please find my check/money order for $8.00 to cover the cost of my report

(enclosed is a copy of my driver's license or state ID, bill with current address and Social

Security number.

Marcus A. Beasley

CREDIT INVESTIGATION REQUEST FORM
(SAMPLE)

NAME _____

ADDRESS _____

SOCIAL SECURITY # _____

HOME PHONE _____

DATE OF BIRTH _____

SIGNATURE _____ DATE _____

COMPANY NAME _____

ACCOUNT # _____
(CHECK ONE)

NOT MY ACCOUNT _____

NEVER LATE _____

PAID IN FULL _____

PAID BEFORE COLLECTION/CHARGE-OFF _____

IN BANKRUPTCY _____

OTHER _____

Use this form when there are inaccuracies on your credit report.

NEGOTIATING WITH CREDITORS

Sometimes we as believers face adverse situations and circumstances that hinder our ability to pay our bills on time. In this situation we need to consider the parable of the unjust steward. In Luke 16:1–8, Jesus tells us the parable of the unjust steward. The parable goes on to say that the unjust steward had to account for his master's possessions. In verses 3–6 the steward realizes that he must provide for his future livelihood. The Bible says that he was too old for hard physical labor and was too proud to beg; so he developed a scheme in which he could win friends in his time of need. So he decided to ask his master's debtors how much they owed. When the one debtor replied a hundred measures of oil, the steward told him to pay fifty. Another debtor owed a hundred measures of wheat, the steward told him to pay eighty. What the steward did was to negotiate wisely with his master's debtors to settle the accounts. The steward sacrificed current gain for future security. In looking at this we as believers must understand that although our future is not on earth, we can financially prepare a very secure retirement future by negotiating to eliminate debt. Consider the following steps in negotiating with your creditors:

- Go over your budget and determine an affordable payment plan for all of your creditors (do this when you cannot meet the minimum payments)
- Contact your creditors
- Explain your situation honestly
- Try to speak with supervisors (record names of everyone you speak with, also dates and times)
- Negotiate (ask God to allow negotiation)
- Get confirmation of your agreements (ask for them to be sent in writing before you make payments)
- Follow up letter indicating agreement (thank the creditor)

Most creditors are understanding and are willing to negotiate with you. Keep in mind that the creditors want to collect the debt just as much as you want to eliminate the debt.

REESTABLISHING YOUR GOOD CREDIT FILE

In order for us to reestablish an excellent credit file we must create a history of making payments on time. We want the issuers of credit to recognize a pattern of consistent payments. The following is steps in building a good credit file:

- Establish a good relationship with a bank or credit union.

Make sure you record all purchase transactions and write checks responsibly.

Bounced checks will result in negative consequences. Inform bank or credit union your intention to rebuild your credit portfolio.

- Pay all bills on time.

Develop payment schedules for all of your bills.

- Apply and receive a secured credit card by opening a savings account.

Most financial institutions will give you 1.5 times your deposit. Use your account and after 31 days pay the credit card in full. Even with a $0 balance allow it to remain open because this will increase your credit score.

- Open a savings account at your financial institution. Two weeks later ask for a secured loan based on your savings account deposit. Go to three other financial institutions and do the same thing. Thirty-one days after you borrow from the first institution, pay back the money. Do the same thing at the three other institutions. This will show up as an R1 on your credit report four times. For example: deposit in bank 1 $500 savings and borrow $500 dollars secured by savings account. Deposit in bank 2, then borrow, deposit in bank 3, borrow and deposit in bank 4, then borrow. After 31 days in bank 1 pay back loan, then do the same at banks 2, 3, and 4. (Close all accounts.) Make sure you ask the banks if they will do a hard inquiry on your credit report. If they say yes, then find a lending institution that will not.

- Keep debt ratio under 20% of income

- Stability is very important to creditors so decide to live at your current residence and maintain your present employment for at least two years.

- Do not apply for additional or new credit for two years.

- Have no more than two credit cards

- Keep credit card balances below credit limits.

- Close all nonactive accounts with zero balances.

- Review credit reports twice a year.

It is very important to maintain discipline and determination in building your credit file. In order to experience financial freedom we first have to reestablish our good credit name, learn how to manage debt and understand how to multiply money.

CHAPTER 5

FINANCIAL PLANNING & DEBT

We must as believers align ourselves with people that have a good understanding of economics and finances. Partnering ourselves with financial advisors is wise and it makes good financial sense. Even God's word tells us in Proverbs 1:5, "A wise man will hear, and will increase learning; and a man of understanding shall attain unto wise counsels." In addition to seeking wise counsel, we must be more productive after we come home from our jobs. We must increase our knowledge of economics and finances; we accomplish this by reading. We cannot afford to have the spirit of entertainment dominate our lives in the evening. If we want something we never had before we are going to have to do something we have never done.

Before we get into the heart of our financial planning, we need to first prioritize our financial plan. There are three levels of our financial destinies, two of which involve planning and the third in which we reap the benefits of our financial plan. The three levels are:

1. **Basic Financial Needs. Level 1 (security level)**

    a) home

    b) planning & forecasting

    c) budget, credit and debt strategies

    d) life insurance

    e) disability insurance

    f) college funding

    g) retirement planning

    h) emergency fund

    i) long-term care planning

    j) estate planning

The key here is to complete each of the above items before moving to level 2.

2. **Risk. Level 2 (investment level)**

    a) stocks/bonds

    b) mutual funds

    c) annuities

    d) variable insurance products

    e) tax lien/tax deeds

    f) pre-foreclosures (real estate)

g) foreclosures

h) commodities

i) IPOs (initial public offering)

This is a significant level that creates financial freedom and wealth. The key to understand about this level is the word risk. If you have a low-risk philosophy and lifestyle you will not experience financial freedom. The higher the degree of risk, the greater the returns. Consequently, the lower degree of risk, the lower the return. If your degree of risk is low then you are not stepping out in faith because low-risk living does not require faith. Low-risk living can result in prayerlessness because you do not need God to intervene in your financial situation. In the case of Peter seeing Jesus walking on the water, if he had a low-risk attitude he would have never attempted to walk on the water to meet Jesus. Instead, he stepped out on faith and actually walked on water. Also, when he took his focus off Jesus he began to sink, but Jesus still reached out His hand and pulled him up. Jesus will do the same for us when we hit the financial doldrums; he will pull us up. It is then and only then that our faith is exercised because at that point our total reliance is on the Lord and not we ourselves. **INCREASE THE RISK IN YOUR LIVES TO SHOW THE LORD THAT YOUR FAITH IS IN HIM.**

3. **Level 3 (toys)**

   a) racehorses

   b) yachts

   c) aircraft

   d) houses

This is the play-hard level in which total financial freedom is experienced. It takes hard work and dedication to make this level happen.

BUDGETING & DEBT ELIMINATION

Budgeting is critically important because before you can begin to eliminate your debt you must first have a clear understanding of exactly where your money is going. Keep in mind you want to have a complete financial road map to take you to financial freedom and prosperity. In this section there are forms to track your daily spending habits, weekly spending habits and monthly spending habits. There is also a personal debt elimination form to assist in the quest for debt-free living. The goal is to spend 10% of your gross income to **TITHES**, 15% of your net income for **SAVINGS** and 75% of your net income to **DEBT** (includes mortgage or rent, credit cards, loans and car payment). The only other fixed expense will be taxes on your pay. However, if you increase your exemptions you will pay less taxes and have more take-home pay. The other expenses are controllable expenses and we need to discipline ourselves to stay within the predetermined guidelines of our income.

The following is a guideline for the 75% monthly expenditures:

1. 30% of your net income for total mortgage expense (includes insurance, taxes and maintenance)
2. 20% of your net income for nonmortgage expenses (includes car loans and all other loans, credit cards, revolving charges)
3. 15% of your net income to miscellaneous expenses.(includes food, gas, toiletries, personal expenses, etc.)

To illustrate let's look at the following example of a typical family with earnings of $3,000 per month or $36,000 per year (almost the national average of American family income).

$3,000 gross income	25% taxes (gross)	$750
		$2,250 net
	10% tithes (gross)	$300
		$1,950
	15% savings (net)	$337.50
		$1,612.50
	30% mortgage expense (net)	$675
		$937.50
	20% nonmortgage expenses	$450
		$487.50
	15% misc. expenses (net)	$337.50
		$150 positive

DAILY SPENDING FORM

Day_____Date_____

Purchase/ Description   Amount

_____

_____

_____

_____

_____

_____Total_____

Use this form to track your daily spending. If you have a problem spending area this form will be a tremendous benefit to you.

PLANNING & FORECASTING

Successful people have a common thread, and that thread is they all planned their success. Many of us as believers have a vision and a plan but we have not done what God's word has instructed us to do.

In Habakkuk 2:2–3 it says, "Write the vision, and make it plain upon tables, that he may run that readeth it. For the vision is yet for an appointed time, but at the end it shall speak, and not lie: though it tarry, wait for it; because it will surely come, it will not tarry." Remember we talked earlier about the triune nature of God; it is evident in natural manifestation as well. We are instructed to first **write** the vision and make it plain (easily understood) that whoever reads may **run** (action word synonymous with work in this text) and in the end it shall **speak** (manifest itself). We see the words write, run and speak in this text and see that the Lord clearly points out to us what is needed for natural manifestation in our lives as believers. In addition, we need to revisit God's plan as an example. Let's consider the Old Testament as it prophesies the coming of Christ. This is God's way of writing the vision and making it plain. God then sends His Son Jesus to come into the world and complete His earthly ministry (run with God's vision). Jesus then dies for our redemption and reconciliation with the Father and we then receive the Comforter (manifestation). It thus stands to reason that planning is a critical element in the restoration of our finances.

The steps in planning involve short term (one month to two years), medium term (two to five years) and long term goals (five-plus years). Develop your finances around concrete time frames. Please be honest with yourselves by creating realistic and attainable goals.

DEBT DANGER SIGNALS

If you are currently experiencing any of the following scenarios **you have a problem with debt.**

- **You have more month than money.**
- **You worry about money all the time.**
- **You continue to purchase via credit cards.**
- **You purchase necessities with credit cards.**
- **You constantly are asking friends for money.**
- **You make cash advances on credit cards to pay other credit cards.**
- **You never balance your checkbook.**
- **You only pay the minimums on all of your debts.**
- **You apply for new loans to pay off old ones.**
- **You postdate checks.**

- **You struggle to pay your mortgage.**
- **You split bills into two payments (half one month and half next month).**
- **You work three jobs just to make ends meet**
- **You take money from savings to pay bills**
- **You reduce your 401(k) or 403(b) contributions to pay bills.**
- **You stop going to the doctor or dentist because you cannot afford to.**
- **You stop making repairs on your home because you cannot afford to.**

If you find yourself in one or more of these situations, you have joined the problematic debt club. Millions of Americans (including the body of Christ) have a problem with debt. The key is to understand where you are and decide to **ATTACK DEBT.**

DETERMINING YOUR DEBT RATIO

The financial industry believes that if you are spending more than 20% of your after-tax income on nonmortgage debt you are on your way to become indebted. Let's determine how to find our debt ratio.

- **List all of your credit cards, auto loans, school loans and personal loans (do not enter mortgage or rent).**
- **List your monthly payment for each account. Add up all of the payments.**
- **Divide your average monthly debt by your take-home pay (the answer is your nonmortgage percentage of debt).**

Look at the following debt ratio chart to determine where you are.

10%–14% Good credit manager

15%–19% Start evaluating your situation (approaching danger zone)

20%–25% You have a problem with debt

25% plus You need to seek professional help

WEEKLY SPENDING FORM

Week of _____

	Purchase	Sun.	Mon.	Tue.	Wed.	Thurs.	Fri.	Sat.
1								
2								
3								
4								
5								
6								
7								
8								
9								
10								
11								
12								

Use this form to track your weekly spending. You can use the daily spending record to get your weekly totals.

IMPULSE BUYING FORM

ITEMS PURCHASED	AMOUNT	DATE	TOTAL

This form is used to track impulse buying and determine if you need to practice self-control and implement discipline in any one area.

DEBT ELIMINATION PLAN

COMPANY OWED	INTEREST AMOUNT	PAYOFF AMOUNT	#PAYMENTS LEFT	MONTHLY PAYMENT	DUE DATE

This form is used to record those debts that you have identified as short- and medium-range debts you want to eliminate.

DEBT CONSOLIDATION

According to financial statistical data the average American family has almost 9 credit cards and an average balance of $5,000-plus. In addition, credit card interest rates are approaching the 20% level, creating a nation of indebted people. This is a tremendous opportunity for the body of Christ to become debt-free and through the power of God's word minister to the lost regarding their finances and win them to the body.

If you are in major debt the thought of consolidating your debt into one payment may seem awfully attractive. However, this could also work as a negative if you have not controlled your spending. In fact, this can be very dangerous if you are trading unsecured debt for secured debt because if you ever get into a financial bind you could lose your home, car and other critical assets. Consider these simple rules for debt consolidation:

- Never refinance unsecured debt into secured debt.
- Never refinance your car loan into your mortgage loan.
- Stop taking on additional debt (stop spending).
- Consider a consumer counseling service (only the ones that do not charge a fee).
- Always consider interest rates, fees and penalties when considering refinancing

TYPES OF CONSOLIDATION LOANS

- **Low interest rate credit cards**

  If you have a high interest rate credit card you may receive an offer from other credit cards to have a reduced interest rate for an introductory period. Unfortunately, these periods only last for a few months, not long enough for you to pay off the debt.

- **Bill consolidation loans**

  This can be a very effective way to control your finances if you can obtain a loan with a lower interest rate than the rate you are paying on your credit cards.

- **Home equity loans**

  These loans can help lower the interest rate that you are currently paying on your debt. However, you must use your home as collateral. (Be careful.) The other benefit is the interest paid on these loans are tax-deductible.

MONTHLY CASH FLOW & EXPENSE FORM

GROSS INCOME

Salary _____

Bonuses _____

Commission _____

Other Income _____

Total Income _____

SUBTRACT

Taxes _____

Tithes _____

Total _____

EXPENSES

HOUSING

Mortgage or rent _____

Insurance _____

Taxes _____

Telephone _____

Electric _____

Gas _____

Water _____

Maintenance _____

Other Expenses _____

Total _____

AUTOMOBILE(S)

Payments _____

Insurance _____

License/Taxes _____

Maint./Repair _____

Total _____

CLOTHING _____

SAVINGS _____

ENTERTAINMENT

Vacation _____

Baby Sitter _____

Other _____

Total _____

MEDICAL EXPENSES

Doctor _____

Dentist _____

Other _____

Total _____

CHILD CARE/ SCHOOL

Tuition _____

Transportation

Supplies _____

Day Care _____

Total _____

MISC

Laundry _____

Toiletries _____

Beauty _____

Cash _____

Gifts _____

Other _____

Total _____

FOOD	_____	**INVESTMENTS**	_____
DEBTS		**TOTAL EXPENSES**	_____
Credit Cards	_____		
Loans	_____	**SUBTRACT EXPENSES FROM**	
Other	_____		
Life	_____	**NET INCOME**	_____
Total	_____		
		TOTAL	_____
INSURANCE	_____		
Health	_____		
Other	_____		
Total	_____		

The idea is to have more money than month. If the total number at the bottom is a negative number you need to reevaluate your budget and spending. You should plug the weekly spending form numbers into your monthly cash flow and expense form.

PERSONAL SPENDING GAME PLAN

This form will be used to analyze your spending versus cash flow form to determine if you are overspending in any one particular area.

SPENDING IN THE MONTH OF _____,20_____

WEEK	1	2	3	4	5	ACTUAL	PLAN	DIFF
Electricity								
Gas								
Telephone								
Maintenance								
Credit Cards								
Babysitter								
Vacation								
Doctor								
Dentist								
Toiletries								
Beauty								
Lunch								
Gifts								
Cash								
School								
Transportation								
Cell phone								
Clothes								
Fast food								
Entertainment								
Groceries								
Misc.								

Note: These are items that are considered controllable expenses.

GET OUT OF DEBT NOW

Of all the topics in this book it is my sincerest prayer that the body of Christ take heed to getting out of debt. When we consider the rule of 72 (compound interest) and its effect on money we must also understand the impact it has on debt. For example, let's say you owe $10,000 and you are paying 18% interest on the debt. If you divide 72 by 18 that answer is 4. Every four years the interest amount will double on the unpaid principle.. Now ask yourselves a question: in the four years when your debt doubles will your salaries double as well? Probably not. This is extremely important for us to understand if we are going to get out and stay out of debt. Remember saints, a simple law of economics is you cannot spend more than you make; at some point it will overtake you financially. Another important factor is when we get out of debt, what we own we own rather than the lender owning it.

It is entirely possible for us to get out of debt; all we need to do is to make up our minds and allow God's word to govern our decisions. Remember, it is in the interest of the world to keep us indebted and continually borrowing money to enslave us physically and mentally. Proverbs 27:12 says, "A prudent man foresees evil and hides himself; the simple pass on and are punished."

There are several strategies I want to introduce to you to reduce your debt. If you have a fixed rate of interest on any debt you have (your house, etc.) this can reduce your debt from 30 years to 19. Ask your mortgage company to send you a copy of your amortization schedule for the debt you have with them. When you receive the schedule it will show you the amount of your payment going to principal and interest. For example, look at your schedule for the month of September. Let's say your payment is $750 per month of which $600 goes to interest and $150 goes to principal; now look at the next month's (October) principal amount, let's say $150; what you should do in your September payment is to send a $750 and a $150 check marked "for principal only." What you have done is to pay down that principal amount, thereby making your payoff 10–12 years sooner. Continue to repeat this month after month.

Another strategy to use is to have a biweekly mortgage payment program set up through your bank or financial institution. If your financial institution does not have this program there are companies that will set up this process with your financial institution. What you are doing is to create two additional payments per year, reducing the number of years by 10–12.

You can use this same strategy with your credit cards and any outstanding debt. The purpose is to reduce the length of time of payoff.

We must get out of debt now because of this administration's decision to spend our tax dollars for war (not a political statement). In the coming years our national debt will exceed $485 trillion dollars. How do we think the deficit will be reduced? Yes, you are correct if you said by increasing our taxes and/or cutting many of our social programs. Either way we the consumers lose. In addition, we have not even considered inflation which will continually erode the purchasing power of the dollar. It is critically important for us to not only get out of debt now but to also teach our children the significance of not getting themselves into debt.

CHAPTER 6

INVESTING YOUR MONEY WISELY

INTEREST, TIME,RISK, DIVERSIFICATION, ASSET ALLOCATION, COSTS,TAXES, INFLATION

- MUTUAL FUNDS
- ANNUITIES
- VARIABLE UNIVERSAL LIFE INSURANCE
- DISABILITY INSURANCE
- LONG-TERM CARE INSURANCE
- COLLEGE FUNDING
- EMERGENCY FUNDING
- 401(K), 403(B) AND 457 RETIREMENT PLANS
- IRAS (TRADITIONAL & ROTH)

DIVERSIFICATION

Diversification is one of the most important keys of investing. There are many investment philosophies available to investors. Experience has taught me that it is absolutely critical in allocating your assets between different asset classes, fund styles and types. For example, having a mixture of growth, specialty, aggressive growth, bonds, lifestyle funds (stocks and bonds combined) and value funds makes an impressive allocation model. Of course this depends on your risk tolerance, time horizon and investment objectives. Many 401(k) and 403(b) portfolios I've seen are invested primarily in S&P 500 companies. However, the Russell 2000 (small cap index) has outperformed the large cap index(S&P 500) over the course of seventy-five years of the investment markets.

To illustrate my point even further, our God advises us in the art of diversification through the wisest man to ever live, Solomon. In Ecclesiastes 11:2 Solomon says, "Give a portion to **seven, and to eight;** for thou knowest not what evil shall be upon the earth." The most important key here is to invest in several interests so that if one fails the others will be able to carry on the portfolio. In addition, if we carefully look at the end of this verse, it talks about the unknown evil which may exist on the earth; diversification helps in preparing for the unknown inevitable calamities and trials that come to the sons of men (such as corporate accounting scandals).

Let's take a look at how diversification works in our favor:

Investment 1

$50,000 investment in year 1 in one company at 8% for 30 years: you would have $503,132.

Investment 2

$50,000 investment = $10,000 at 15%, $10,000 at 10%, $10,000 at 5%, $10,000 at 0% and $10,000 loss. $10,000 at 15% for 30 years = $662,118, $10,000 at 10% for 30 years = $174,494, $10,000 at 5% for 30 years = $43,219 and $10,000 at 0% = $10,000 and a $10,000 loss. You will have after 30 years $889,831.

DOLLAR COST AVERAGING

Dollar cost averaging is a very important concept for us to understand regarding our investment strategies and approach. Many of us really panic when we see a continual decline in the market. We do all sorts of things including taking our money out of the market and putting it in a fixed account, discontinuing contributions to our retirement plan until the market rebounds or surrendering our accounts to put the money in the bank.(we accept the 10% penalty and pay ordinary income taxes on our money). If you are guilty in taking one of the above actions I want to change your mindset and your understanding of how the dollar cost averaging concept will benefit you in the long run.

Let's take a look at how this works: The unit value of a fund in January is $10.00 per share. You are contributing $100 per month into this fund. You will purchase 10 shares in January. ($100/10 per share = 10 shares). At the end of 12 months you will have 120 shares with a value of $1,200. Keep in mind if the unit value increases the quantity of shares you purchase monthly will decline.

Let's look at a volatile market; let's say the unit value in January is $10.00 per share and you contribute $100 per month. The market then goes down and your unit value declines to $5.00 per share. In January you purchased 10 shares and in February you purchase 20 shares. Then in July, the unit value falls to $2 per share; you now purchase 50 shares. Then in December the unit value returns to $10 per share. Let's see how we did: Jan. 10 shares, Feb. 20 shares, Mar. 20 shares, Apr. 20 shares, May 20 shares, Jul. 20 shares, Jul. 50 shares, Aug. 50 shares, Sept. 50 shares, Oct. 50 shares, Nov. 50 shares and Dec. 10 shares. We now have a total of 370 shares @ $10 share in Dec. = $3,700. Do you see how a volatile market can actually benefit us? We should praise God in times of a bear market and truly rejoice because we now understand what God is planning to do and that is to multiply our money through the famine that He created for our benefit. **TRUST HIM.**

401(k)/ 403(b)/ 457

Whether your company is for profit or nonprofit, most employers offer a voluntary contribution to a 401(k), 403(b) or government 457 plan. I want to convey a very important point when addressing this issue. It is critically important for the saints to take full advantage of this opportunity.

When looking at retirement, think of it as a three-legged stool in which the pension, social security and your voluntary contributions will fund your retirement. Most pension plans will replace only about 50% of what you currently make and Social Security (full benefit) will replace 15–20%. Adding these two together we can see only a 70% replacement. Remember, most financial experts agree that you need at least 85% replacement to have an average retirement. If we do the math we can see we have an income gap of 15%. If your pension replaces less than 50% your gap will be even larger. It is important to contribute as much as possible into retirement plans because:

1. **Contributions reduce gross income, saving on taxes**
2. **Contributions are pre-tax (allowing for full amount to be contributed)**
3. **We have total control of portfolio**
4. **There are both variable and fixed investments**
5. **Plans offer professional money management**
6. **Plans offer tax-deferred growth**

Some employers even make matching contributions to a certain amount of money based on what you (the employee) contribute.

In 2005 the government allows a contribution of $14,000 and an additional catch-up provision of $4,000 if you are age 50. In 2006 that contribution limit will be $15,000. You should fully maximize contributions before considering buying any other type of investments.

As with IRAs there are distribution rules that apply. You must be age 59 1/2 before receiving a distribution from a 403(b), 401(k) and a government 457 plan or pay a 10% penalty tax. Like IRAs there are exclusions. They are:

- First-time home buyers
- Education expenses
- Medical expenses

You are eligible to make withdrawals under the following circumstances:

1. Age 59 1/2 or older
2. Separation from service
3. Death or disability

You can keep your money in the plan until age 70 1/2; at that time if you do not have earned income you must take a minimum distribution or pay a huge penalty tax up to 50%.

Since the contributions are pre-tax you will incur ordinary income taxes upon distribution of your account. Consult with your tax advisor regarding distributions.

Make sure your investment advisor does an asset allocation builder to determine how to distribute the assets in the portfolio. When choosing your funds it is very important to have representation in all three asset classes; large, mid- and small cap funds. It is critically important to see your investment advisor at least once per year.

Mutual Funds

More than 7 trillion dollars is invested in mutual funds in the United States. Much of this money found its way into funds in the past 10 years. Because of such an increase, there is a demand for information about mutual funds for the small investor. The purpose of this information is to familiarize you with terms and processes involving mutual funds so you will have a better understanding

Definition of a Mutual Fund

A mutual fund is a pool of investments used to buy a large portfolio of securities that is managed by a professional money manager. When we buy a share in a mutual fund, we buy a piece of each security held in the fund's portfolio. Mutual funds are referred to as "investment companies" whose shares are sold to the public and which invest the proceeds of these sales in other public companies.

Risk

There are risk associated with the purchase of a mutual fund. Even if we have a portfolio that consist only of guaranteed U.S. government bonds, it contains an element and degree of risk. It is very important for you to remember that the risk of total loss is lessened by diversification in the portfolio through properly allocating your assets in different asset classes and sectors within those asset classes.

Terms

Debt Security. This is a security such as a bond or debenture, in which a specific amount is owed to the purchaser of the security. Also called fixed-income assets.

Equity Security. Security such as a common or preferred stock in which the purchaser of the security purchases a piece of the company and is an owner of the company.

Issuer. This is the entity from which the security is derived. Mutual funds are the issuers of their shares or units.

Government Backed or Guaranteed. The U.S. government guarantees its bonds and will pay the amount shown on the face of the bond. However, this does not guarantee that the market price will remain constant. It is because of this that government securities will fluctuate in value. Interest rates and the prices of existing bonds move in opposite directions.

Interest/principal. The principal is the amount you invest. Interest represents your earnings.

Types of Funds

Mutual funds are either closed-end or open-end. A closed-end fund issues only a certain number of shares. After the shares are sold and the money is invested in its portfolio of securities, trading of the fund's shares can take place. The company is not obligated to redeem its shares or issue more shares. An investor who no longer wants to hold the shares may sell them in the market. An open-end mutual fund is constantly offering new shares to the public and redeeming its outstanding shares. There is no limit to the number of shares that can be issued.

Many mutual funds charge a sales fee or commission, which is known as a "load." This fee varies from fund to fund, but is usually in the range of 3 to 8% of the purchase price, with most funds charging about 5%. Some funds do not charge this fee; these funds are known as "no load" funds. All funds pay continuing management fees of different amounts to their advisors. It is critically important that you compare both the load and the management fees to determine which will provide a better return over the time you expect to hold the shares. Some funds also charge an exit or sales fee which may cut the return to shareholders. Finally, because 12b-1 plans backload the fees and are based on the average value of the fund, 12b-1 plans may also reduce the return to shareholders.

Balanced mutual funds are funds composed of both common stocks (equities) and fixed income securities (bonds or debentures). The objective of this type of investment is to minimize the risk without sacrificing the possibilities of long-term growth. These funds invest their money in specified proportions, in fixed income securities and common stocks. To give you an example of how this works, a portfolio may tell you that 50% of its assets invest in common stock and 50% of its assets invest in fixed income securities.

Growth and income funds are for those who want income and whose goal is not immediate capital gain. These funds specialize in high-yield stocks and bonds. These types of investment plans have two objectives: to achieve long-term growth of capital and to provide investors with a reasonable level of current income. Income funds usually emphasize common stocks, favoring those that pay dividends. In declining markets, growth and income funds may show a somewhat higher degree of price stability than funds oriented toward capital gains. However, they may also advance at a slower rate in a rising market.

A dual purpose fund invests equal dollar amounts in each of two types of shares, income and capital. Income shareholders receive a set, minimum rate of return and are paid all of the dividend and interest income (less expenses) produced by the fund. Income shares are redeemable at a stated time and price. Income shareholders do not receive any part of the fund's capital growth. Capital shareholders, on the other hand, receive no periodic income, but are entitled to all the company's assets after the company terminates and the income shareholders have been reimbursed.

Bond funds invest in debt securities, usually in either corporate or government bonds. These funds are generally exposed to less risk than others. Since risk is commensurate with the potential for gain, these investments are not likely to provide exceptional income or gain. While these funds are conservative, they are subject to at least three potential risks:

1. The market value of debt instruments fluctuates, so that the value of your shares will fluctuate. Your income may be relatively stable and the underlying obligations may be guaranteed, but that will not help you if you need to liquidate your shares quickly in an emergency and the market is down.

2. The bonds could be called, removing a source of income from the fund. You may also receive back a portion of your principal when bonds are called, so it is important to have a reinvestment system in place if you invest in a bond fund.

3. The quality of the underlying bonds may not be very high, and the value of the bonds may decline or the bonds may actually default. Make sure you check the restrictions on the quality of the bonds in which the manager may invest. A diversified portfolio lessens the risk.

Option funds are high-risk investments in which the manager of the fund buys and sells securities options and engages in "short" sales (sales of securities one does not own). The potential for return is great, but so is the **RISK.**

Sector portfolio funds invest in the securities in a particular industry. Examples include an oil and gas income fund, which holds a portfolio of interest in oil and gas wells, or a gold fund, which invest in gold mining company stock. There are also funds that invest in only low-grade bonds, high-yield money market instruments or bank certificates of deposit.

Mutual funds may offer taxable or tax-free income. Changes in the tax laws have narrowed the options for investors to shelter investment income from taxes. However, you can still invest in municipal bonds or tax-exempt notes. These mutual funds may be exempt from federal income taxes, but they may be subject to state and local taxes. There are some funds that are income producing that are exempt from taxes in certain states. Tax-exempt funds are typically identified as "municipal bond" funds or "tax-free" funds.

Fees

Management fees are paid to fund administrators for their professional advice and are usually computed by taking a certain percentage of the total value of the assets, usually less than one percent.

Custodian fees are paid to trustees or directors of an institution that holds all the assets of the mutual fund.. This is usually a small fee, about 1/10 of 1%.

Sales charges (sales commission) can range from 1 to 8% of the amount you have to invest in the fund. Some funds reduce the percentage if you invest a greater amount in the fund. Your broker should be able to show you how much the sales charges are.

Contingent deferred sales charges are levied to discourage movement in and out of the funds. Generally between 1 and 5% of the redemption amount, they apply for 1–5 years following the initial purchase and are usually on a declining scale.

12-B1 plans allow fees to be assessed over the life of the investment to compensate the distributor of the fund. These funds range from .25 to 1.25% of the average net asset value per year.

Investigate Before You invest

Before you invest it is very important to know your investment goals and objectives. Before you choose a fund establish your own financial goals, decide how much risk you can afford to take, your time horizon, services and track record of the mutual fund.

It is critically important to obtain and read the fund's prospectus. A prospectus is a document given to potential investors in connection with a public offering of securities. It is a written statement of all relevant information about the company, such as its history, operations, financial conditions and key personnel. Mutual funds are required by law to provide prospectuses. Most include a description of the fund, a summary of the financial structure and operations, description of the fund's assets, the management structure, salaries of officers, the expenses of the offering and specific uses of the proceeds.

The prospectus also contains investment objectives of the fund. The success of the fund is measured by how well the fund achieves its stated objectives. Some of the most common objectives are "conservation of capital," "growth" or "income." When you consider investing in a fund you should first consider the fund's investment objective. The fund objective should correspond with your own objective and ability to tolerate risk associated with those objectives. In addition, make sure you know all of the fees involved with the fund and its historical returns in one-, five-, and ten-year averages.

Net Asset Value

The net asset value is the present dollar value of each share. The fund uses this amount when redeeming (or selling) shares. It is determined by totaling the market value of all securities owned by the fund and subtracting all its liabilities. The balance is divided by the number of the fund's outstanding shares. The result is the net asset value/share. The net asset value is computed at least daily to keep investors constantly informed of the value of their holdings.

Voluntary Accumulation Plans

These are investment programs that enable customers to purchase small quantities of mutual fund shares on a regular basis. An account can be opened with a minimum, predetermined investment of cash or mutual fund shares. You can make additional deposits on a regular basis, usually monthly or quarterly, with which fund shares are purchased on your behalf.

IRAS (TRADITIONAL & ROTH)

IRAs are retirement vehicles designed to close the income gap between pension and Social Security benefits. Financial experts agree that you will need at least 85% of your pre-retirement income to retire comfortably. Almost anyone with earned income can open an IRA, even if they are contributing to an employer-sponsored retirement program. IRA's offer tax-deferred growth and the traditional IRA offers tax-deductible contributions depending on your income level.

TRADITIONAL IRA

Most people are familiar with the traditional IRA. If you are under 70 ½ and have earned income, you are eligible to participate in an IRA. In 2005 you are allowed to contribute $4,000 and if you are age 50 an additional $500 catch-up provision is allowed.

If you are single and your income is less than $40,000 in 2005 your contributions are fully tax-deductible; if your income is greater than $50,000 in 2005 your contributions are not tax-deductible. In 2005 if you are married filing jointly and your income is less than $60,000 your contributions are fully tax-deductible; if your income exceeds $70,000 your contributions are not tax-deductible. In 2005 if you are single and make less than $45,000, your contributions are fully tax deductible; if your income exceeds $55,000 your contributions are not tax-deductible. In 2005 if you are married filing jointly and your income is less than $65,000 your contributions are fully tax-deductible; if your income exceeds $75,000 your contributions are not tax-deductible.

In order to access your money penalty-free you must be age 59 ½ or meet one of the following circumstances:

- Qualifying first time home buyer
- Qualifying education expense
- Death or disability
- Reimbursement for certain health expenses
- Selection of substantially equal periodic payments over life expectancy

ROTH IRA

If your income levels exceed the Traditional IRA criteria you may want to consider purchasing a Roth IRA. Your contributions to a Roth IRA are not tax-deductible but the Roth IRA provides for tax-free and penalty-free distributions after five years under the following conditions:

- Age 59 1/2
- Qualified first-time home buyer
- Death or disability

Roth IRAs are not subject to minimum distribution rules like the Traditional IRA. With a Roth IRA you can leave your money in past age 70 1/2 and continue to contribute after age 70 1/2 if you have earned income.

If you are married filing jointly and your income is between 0 to $150,000 you are allowed to contribute up to $4,000 annually. If you make over $160,000 you are not eligible to contribute. If you are single and earn 0 to $95,000 you can contribute up to $4,000 annually. If you earn over $110,000 you are not eligible to contribute.

VARIABLE ANNUITIES

A Variable Annuity is used as a retirement vehicle. Unlike a mutual fund, the variable annuity has a tax-deferred feature which takes full advantage of compounding over time. The variable annuity is dependent on the mutual funds in the annuity contract.

The major benefit of a variable annuity is that in the event of death, the beneficiaries receive a guaranteed death benefit. Unlike an insurance policy, there are no physical examinations and blood tests. In addition, there are no minimum or maximum investment amounts in the variable annuity contract.

The guaranteed death benefit is illustrated as follows: Let's say you invest $50,000 in a variable annuity; soon after the market declines, and your investment is now worth $25,000. In the event of your untimely death the insurance company will pay your beneficiaries $50,000.

Another feature of the variable annuity is that the mutual funds are in a separate account from the general assets of the insurance company. In the event of an insurance company having financial problems, the creditors of the insurance company are not allowed access to the separate account.

The variable annuity also allows tax-free switching between mutual funds. In addition, you have complete control of fund selection, diversification feature with many fund families and professional money management.

The variable annuity tax structure is unique. You pay no taxes on your contributions but have what is called a cost basis (principal). You pay taxes on any appreciation in your account. It is taxed on the LIFO (Last In First Out) method. Consult your tax advisor.

Their are three types of withdrawal methods from a variable annuity:

- Lump sum withdrawals

- Annuitization

- Systematic withdrawals

When accessing your variable annuity money, consult a tax advisor for the best possible scenario based on your financial situation and tax bracket. Your basic choices are:

- Gift the assets to beneficiaries

- Annuitize and tax defer (irrevocable process once selected)

- Take a lump sum and pay taxes

- Make systematic withdrawals (tremendous flexibility)

VARIABLE UNIVERSAL LIFE INSURANCE

The best kept secret in America is the variable universal life insurance policy. This is a permanent insurance policy that is well suited for families that have some assets and enough cash flow to afford the policy. This policy incorporates insurance protection and subaccounts investing in actively managed mutual funds. In addition to the tax-deferred feature of this policy, the cash value accumulation can be borrowed on a tax-free basis. The underlying subaccounts are invested in a separate account apart from the general assets of the insurance company. Depending on your risk tolerance, time horizon and investment style you are in complete control of choosing your portfolio.

The beauty of this policy is it also protects your family in the event of loss. In addition to having a death benefit it has a life benefit. What do I mean, you ask? You can borrow the cash value while still alive and not have to pay back the loan. Remember, the death benefit will pay all policy loans upon the death of the insured. The policy will pay the beneficiaries a tax-free death benefit minus all withdrawals and policy loans. On policy loans, some of the insurance companies will charge 4.75% interest on the loan and then credit 4% of interest on your money allowing you to actually pay .75% interest on the loan.

The two enemies of money are inflation and taxation. According to the wealth formula, money + time +- rate of return – inflation - taxation = wealth. The mutual fund feature of this policy gives us the opportunity to outpace inflation and the tax-free feature of borrowing the accumulated cash allows us to utilize the tax-advantaged part of the policy.

Let's review the important features of this insurance policy:

- Tax-deferred accumulation

- Tax-free switches between mutual funds

- Tax-free loans

- Death benefit payout tax-free to beneficiaries

- Actively managed mutual funds

- Outpacing inflation

- Permanent insurance protection

- Flexible premium payments

Consult your insurance agent or financial advisor about the variable universal life insurance policy. Ask your financial professional for a policy illustration.

HOW MUCH INSURANCE DO I NEED?

D   =   DEBT

I   =   INCOME

M   =   MORTGAGE

E   =   EDUCATION

ADD TOTAL DEBT (EXCLUDE MORTGAGE) + INCOME @ 5 OR 10 YEARS + MORTGAGE + COLLEGE EDUCATION = TOTAL AMOUNT OF INSURANCE NEEDED

DISABILITY INSURANCE

Disability insurance is one of the most critical areas of financial planning because of its effect on other areas of our economic lives. In the event of partial or permanent disability of the breadwinner in a single-income household, the loss of income could be devastating. In a two-income household the same can be said, particularly if the education of children depends on both incomes. Remember when we talked earlier about the security level? It is imperative that college funding and emergency funding are separate accounts. I want to stress the significance of disability insurance because it is just as important as life insurance.

Disability insurance protects assets in the event of loss of income due to any type of disability. Children can still attend college, the mortgage is still paid, cars are still paid and monthly expenditures are met. Disability insurance maximum is based on your current income. Total disability is defined as follows: during your occupational period you are unable to perform substantial and material duties of your occupation and you are not working. Did you know that at any given age the odds of becoming disabled are much higher than dying? Every year at least 12% of the American adult population experiences long-term disability. In addition, one of every seven working adults will suffer a five-year or longer period of disability before the age of 65. If you are in your midthirties, your chance of experiencing short-term disability before 65 is 50%. If you are in your midforties you have a 44% chance of a short-term disability.

With disability policies you will normally receive 50% of your monthly earned income before taxes. When purchasing a disability insurance policy you have four variables to consider: **how much coverage, the definition of disability as defined in the policy, the waiting period before benefits kick in and the length of the benefit period.**

Some benefits in the disability policy are:

- **Capital Sum Benefit**: lump-sum benefit of 12 times maximum monthly benefit helps to adjust financially to a total and irrevocable loss of use without possibility of recovery of sight in one eye or use of hand or foot.

- **Presumptive Benefit:** you will receive full disability benefit if you permanently loose speech, hearing in both ears, sight in both eyes, or use of both hands, both feet, or one hand and one feet. Benefits will be paid as long as loss continues. If benefit period is to age 65 this feature extends to a lifetime.

- **Waiver of Premium:** if you are disabled for the lesser of 90 days or the elimination period your premiums are waived.

- **Death Benefit:** lump-sum benefit of three times your maximum monthly benefit is paid if you die after satisfying the elimination period while receiving benefits.

- **Rehabilitation Benefit:** if you want to pursue a rehabilitation program to return to work, this feature allows an extra benefit to cover the cost of rehabilitation.

In addition, there are some riders you may want to consider when buying disability insurance:

1. **Automatic Benefit Increase:** this rider automatically increases your coverage every year for five years without submitting evidence of insurability

2. **Benefit Update:** allows increase in coverage to maximum amount for which you are eligible every three years without evidence of insurability.

3. **Cost of Living Benefit:** this feature allows your benefit to be adjusted with inflation.

If your employer offers disability insurance you should strongly consider this benefit. If your employer does not, you need an individual policy for you and your spouse if you are a two-income household; if you are single and have children it is a critical insurance policy (just as important as life insurance).

LONG-TERM CARE INSURANCE

IT IS ESTIMATED THAT 43 OUT OF EVERY 100 AMERICANS WILL NEED SOME TYPE OF LONG TERM CARE IN THEIR LIVES. I'm sure you know of a family (maybe your own) where children are taking care of an aging parent. This can be a difficult adjustment for the parent and the children supplying the daily needs of the parents. Long-term care helps with one or more of the activities of daily living (ADLs); these activities include bathing, dressing, transferring, toileting, continence and eating.

Long-term care can be financially devastating for patients and families. How much does it cost, you ask? In 1997 the average cost was over $46,000 for a year in a nursing home. If you could afford a private nurse to visit your home three times a week for about two hours per visit, it would cost almost $20,000. One third of all nursing home costs are paid by patients and their families from their own pocket. Many people sell their lifelong assets such as homes and investments and deplete their savings accounts to pay for long-term care. Many of us are told that Medicare will supply all of our long-term care needs when the truth of the matter is **DO NOT DEPEND ON MEDICARE TO COVER YOUR LONG-TERM CARE NEEDS.** Your question at this point might be, what is the solution? Long-term care insurance is a new kind of insurance introduced in the 1980s as nursing home insurance but has been changed a lot since then. Let's look at some startling statistics:

1. 2.2 million people turned 65 in 1990; 900,000 are expected to enter a nursing home before they die.

2. Women are more likely to need nursing home care than men. 13% of women will spend 5 years in a nursing home. (4% of men will be in for 5 years).

3. The older we get the higher the chance is that we will need care.

Not everyone will be able to afford long-term care insurance. You should not buy long-term care insurance if: you struggle to meet your current monthly obligations, you have limited assets or if Social Security is your only source of income. You should consider buying long term care insurance if you have significant assets you want to protect and you do not want to be a burden on your children financially.

You can purchase long-term care insurance through your local insurance agent or ask your financial advisor, who may sell long-term care insurance. You may be able to purchase a long-term care policy that covers both husband and wife. This type of policy usually involves a total benefit that applies to both individuals on the policy. For example, if the total policy is $200,000 and one spouse uses $50,000, the other $150,000 would be left to pay for the other spouse's care. Insurance companies usually pay benefits using the expense-incurred method or the indemnity method. Most policies use the expense-incurred method of payment, where the insurance company determines policy eligibility for benefits when services are received. The indemnity method involves paying a certain dollar amount. The insurance company determines when you are eligible; the specifics of care are not important

Let's talk about what is covered in a typical long-term care policy. The policy may cover:

1. Nursing home care
2. Home health care
3. Personal care in your home
4. Care in other community facilities
5. Care in assisted living facilities
6. Care in adult day care centers

An important aspect of long-term care policies is that most of them will not pay benefits to family members who provide care in their homes.

Another important aspect of the long-term care policy is what types of facilities are covered under the policy. Most policies cover state-licensed facilities. However, policies will not cover homes for the aged, rest homes and personal care homes. Many policies are very specific in what facilities are covered and will list points about the facilities that are not covered. Remember saints, if you are not placed in the facility that is specified in your policy, your insurance company may not pay benefits.

Of course, there are exclusions . They are:

- Attempted suicide or self-inflicted injuries
- Alcohol or drug addition
- Mental disorder or disease, other than Alzheimer's disease or other dementia
- Illness or injury from war
- Government-provided treatment in a government facility

Policies usually pay benefits by the day, week or the month. To give you an example, an expense-incurred policy may pay a benefit of $125 per day and a weekly benefit of $400. When you purchase a policy you will have the choice of getting $50 to $250 per day or $1,500 to $7,500 a month for nursing home care.

You become eligible for benefits when:

- You can't do 3 of the 6 ADL's
- If you cannot bathe or eat unassisted, under some policies
- You suffer a mental incapacity
- Your doctor orders care

- You are hospitalized

When you decide to buy a long-term care policy, here are some suggestions to include as benefits on your policy:

1. **Inflation Protection**: policy benefit rises with the cost of nursing home care.

2. **Third Party Notice**: this benefit lets you name someone for the insurance company to contact if your coverage is about to end because you forgot to pay the premium.

3. **Waiver of Premium:** this benefit allows you to stop paying premiums once you are in a nursing home and you are receiving benefits.

4. **Restoration of Benefits: this** benefit allows you to keep the maximum amount of your original benefit even after your policy has paid you benefits

5. **Premium Refund at Death:** this benefit pays your estate any premiums you paid minus any benefits the company paid.

There is some additional information you need to know regarding long-term care policies, which concerns nonqualified versus qualified plans and preexisting conditions. Please consult an insurance advisor for additional information.

EMERGENCY FUND

This is one of the most critical areas of our financial lives, emergency fund preparation. This is not a savings or checking account. This money is solely used for unexpected situations that arise. Every family should have 6–12 months' cash reserves set aside (in addition to checking and savings accounts) for emergencies such as major car repairs, major appliance repairs or replacement, unexpected illnesses, job layoffs, investment opportunities and major home repairs or maintenance. There are many vehicles by which to achieve this goal. Financially speaking, you could use a three-, six-, or twelve-month CD or money market securities (check with your local bank). Yes, you can use a bank for liquidity and emergency fund purposes.

COLLEGE FUNDING

In our changing world with a global economy and market, a good college education will be imperative to give our children an opportunity to unlock their potential. It is documented by the College Board that college graduates earn 80% more than high school graduates. It costs students a tremendous amount of money to educate themselves and when they graduate they are in serious debt (because of interest rates). We as believers have to outpace inflation and better prepare financially to send our kids to college. College cost for four-year attendance at a public institution averaged over $38,000 in 2003. The cost of attending a private institution for four years averaged over $100,000 in 2003. What is the answer? A state-sponsored 529 plan. These plans offer a tax-advantaged way to invest to keep up with the rising cost of college. In addition your state may offer additional tax advantages. The features of the 529 plan are: anyone can contribute to the account, you can change beneficiaries as often as you like, you can use the money at any college in the country, you pay no federal income taxes on the earnings, there is a gift tax exclusion (up to $55,000) for five years ($110,000 married couples), and there are estate tax benefits. You can start by contributing as little as $15 per month or as high as $245,000 over the life of the account. The age of your child will determine how you will allocate the assets in your account. The younger your child is the more aggressive your account should be. As your child gets closer to college you will need to become less aggressive and more conservative in your approach toward investing. You have complete control over allocating your assets in the account. Ask your financial advisor about a state-supported 529 college plan.

CHAPTER 7
INCOME OPPORTUNITIES

In the new millennium there are several industries that we can benefit from to create additional income for our families. The phrase I want to convey to the body is called MSI (Multiple Sources of Income). In Ecclesiastes 11:1, it says "Cast thy bread upon the waters; for thou shalt find it after many days." Casting thy bread among the waters could suggest widespread distribution of assets for a generous return in time of harvest. In addition, it could suggest it is wise to have many income streams in the days of famine.

We will consider seven opportunities that can really impact our financial lives and give us multiple sources of income.

1. **Internet/information superhighway**.

   This is a trillion-dollar industry where the marketplace has been upgraded from local to regional, from regional to national, and from national to international. I've come across a unique opportunity involving network marketing, financial services and the power of the Internet. This opportunity costs $30 to join and $19.95 a month. This opportunity helps you to get out of debt and to restore your credit to enhance your borrowing power. In addition, it has a tremendous income opportunity for those who are interested in their own Internet business. Go to www.wealthlink.com/promiselandproperties to review this amazing opportunity.

2. **Prepaid mortgages.**

   There are over 50 million homeowners in this country. In 2002–03 interest rates hit a forty-year low and this prompted millions of homeowners to refinance to reduce their monthly obligations. This opportunity allows you to establish a business designed to help homeowners pay off their mortgages much sooner by paying on a biweekly as opposed to monthly basis.

3. **Nutrition.**

   The world has over 6 billion people, most of who are health-conscious and in pursuit of a longer life. The body contains over 400 muscles, 403 major joints, 206 bones, 14 billion nerve cells, 100 trillion other cells, 300 sweat glands and over 60,000 miles of lymph and blood vessels that are continually subject to pesticides and other artificial ingredients put in our foods .This provides a tremendous opportunity to market health and nutrition products wholesale to customers.

4. **Elderly health care.**

There were 76 million people born between 1946–1964, called the baby boomer generation. In 15 to 25 years the majority of these people will be in retirement. Long-term care statistics tell us that 43 out of every 100 will need care in their retirement. Preparing professionally and getting credentials in elderly health care opens up opportunities such as purchasing a group home and/or adding on to homes to care for clients. I personally know people who do this and earn a handsome salary.

5. **Prepaid legal services.**

Over 50% of Americans are in some type of legal situation. The 50% and climbing divorce rate of 50%, one lawsuit for every three Americans and three court cases filed every second in America provide a tremendous network marketing opportunity for the body of believers.

6. **Pre-foreclosures and foreclosures.**

In 2002 there were over a million foreclosures in America. In 2003 corporate layoffs, dwindling consumer confidence and fear pulling at the hearts of man in the financial markets has contributed to the most lucrative real estate opportunity our country has ever known. Municipality tax sale auctions, sheriff's sales and government auctions have become a gold mine for many investors.

7. **Financial services advisor certification.**

In the next five to twenty years over 10 trillion dollars will be transferred from the baby boomer generation to Generation X. Individuals who get financial services advising professional certifications stand to be paid very well. Financial services companies are also seeking financial advisors to service their existing client base.

CHAPTER 8

THE FINANCIAL PROMISED LAND

We are now going to talk about how to get to the financial promised land without good credit and by using very little money out of your pocket. In addition, we will also discuss very lucrative strategies designed to build wealth for generations and arm the body of Christ with effective ways to gain financial independence. What I'm about to introduce to you I have done for years and have accumulated a large asset base and substantially increased my net worth. If you pay attention and implement the following, you can be financially free in two short years.

What am I talking about, you ask? **REAL ESTATE.** I have no formal training or education in this field but I do have the divine instruction of the Holy Spirit. If God can do it for me He can do it for you because He has no respect of persons. Remember God said in His word according to Proverbs 16:9, "A man's heart plans his way, but the Lord directs his steps." The key words here are plan (we have to do) and direct (what God will do). We must understand what I stated earlier, that God will not plan for us and we cannot direct our own steps. If we do our part God will definitely keep His word and do His part.

If you have the spirit of Joshua and Caleb this will be of interest to you. If you have the spirit of the other 10 spies, then you will continue to wander in the wilderness financially for the rest of your life. It is your decision. What will it be? Let's possess the land.

In this chapter we will concentrate on flipping contracts, flipping properties, buying at tax sales, foreclosure auctions and pre-foreclosures. In addition, we will discuss no-money-down strategies, no credit involved purchases and receiving cash at closing.

The foundation for this teaching is rooted in God's word. In Deuteronomy 8:12 the word of the Lord says, "when you have eaten and are full, and have built beautiful houses and dwell in them." The key word here is houses which is plural. Also, in Acts 4:34, "Nor was there anyone among them who lacked; for all who were possessors of **lands or houses** sold them, and brought the proceeds of the things that were sold." Again we see the words lands and houses in plural form indicating more than one.

FLIPPING CONTRACTS

For the believers who want to add an additional $2,500 to $3,000 to their household without any credit or use of your own money please pay attention. This is a very simple process but it is very effective. First, let's establish some rules to follow.

1. Look for properties for sale by owner.(Make sure seller is motivated. You will see them advertise with words like"must sell, desperate, moving out of town or all offers accepted.")

2. Look for properties that have renters.

3. Make sure the properties are generating cash flow. For example, the mortgage and maintenance is less than what is being paid in rent by tenants.

4. Look for properties located in up-and-coming neighborhoods.

5. Make sure bus routes, main highways, shopping centers, grocery stores, schools and churches are within a two-mile radius of the properties.

6. Look for properties containing amenities such as back yards, fencing, basement, garage etc.

7. Look at current rent levels. (You may be able to raise rents.)

8. Ask if there is an outstanding mortgage balance on each property. If so, make sure it is assumable with low interest rates. If it is not assumable, move on to the next property. FHA loans financed before 1989 are assumable.

9. If properties have no mortgage, that is even better.

10. Look at the maintenance cost of each property.

11. Ask about the reason each property is being sold.

Upon obtaining this information you need to do your homework regarding each particular property. You will need to assess all of the properties in the area and find out the values. You can call realtors and ask for this information and you can go to your state's assessment Web page and find out how much the property was bought for and in what year. The assessment Web page also tells you the square footage, year property was built, the number of total rooms, the number of bedrooms and bathrooms. It will also give you the municipality's assessment value. (this value is not true market value but determines how much in taxes the municipality will receive).

When you have determined a value for a particular property, you want to now develop a price you want to pay to purchase the property. This is most critical in purchasing the property and flipping this contract. Your offer price will be 30 to 40% of the fair market value. Look at the following example: Let's say you find a single-family home for sale by owner. It meets all of the above rules and guidelines set and you do your homework and find out that most of the houses in the area sold for an average of $50,000 for a 3 bedroom, 1 bathroom property. Your offering price will be $32,500, which is 35% off of fair market value. If this is a motivated seller you can do this deal. If this is not acceptable to the seller, you then move on because you must stick to our guidelines to be successful. Let's say the deal is accepted; you must now negotiate an interest rate with the owner. Of course, you are going to negotiate a low rate with low monthly payments and a long 30-year term. For illustrative purposes let's say the rent that the seller is getting is $500 per month. Let's also say hypothetically that your payment to the seller will be $300 per month. Your cash flow is $200 per month.(you are generating $2,400 per year in income.)

You now will put together a contract to present to the seller. Take a look at the following example of a contract you can use:

REAL ESTATE OFFER TO PURCHASE CONTRACT

BE IT KNOWN, the undersigned (your name) (buyer) and/or assigns offers to purchase from (sellers name) (owner) real estate also known as (address of property) in the city or town of (city or town's name), county of (name of county), state of (state's name) said property described as (description of property)

Purchase price	$
Deposit paid	$
Total owed at closing	$

This offer is conditional upon the following terms:

1. **This offer is subject to Buyer obtaining a satisfactory home inspection and pest report within 30 days from date hereof.**

2. **Property is to be sold free and clear of all encumbrances, by good and marketable title, with full possession to said property available to Buyer at date of closing.**

3. **This contract may be assigned; in such event, the Buyer named herein is released of all further liability.**

4. **Buyer is to receive access to property upon acceptance of contract for the purpose of making repairs or showing property to prospective tenants and/or buyers.**

5. **Said property must appraise for at least $_____.**

6. **The closing shall occur on or before _____ at the public recording office, unless such other time and place shall be agreed upon.**

7. **Seller is to make any repairs deemed necessary prior to settlement of this property by Buyer's inspection.**

8. **The parties agree to execute a standard purchase and sales agreement according to the terms of this agreement within _____ days of acceptance of this offer.**

9. This offer is subject to Buyer obtaining financing for no less than $_____ payable over 30 years with interest rate not to exceed _____ % at customary terms with a firm commitment thereto _____ days from date hereof.

10. Contract will be extended for 30 days if necessary.

Signed this _____ day of _____, 20 _____

_____
Buyer   Date

_____
Buyer   Date

_____
Seller   Date

_____
Seller   Date

For the down payment we use what is called a promissory note or a promise to pay at a later date. We never put cash down as a deposit. As you can see this is a no-money-down transaction.

It is critically important for us to include after our name in the section above to include the clause "and/or assigns." This allows us to assign the contract to someone else. This is precisely what we are going to do. After we sign this contract we want to seek another buyer. Remember, we purchased this property for $32,500 so we want to mark up the contract to $37,000. We then advertise the property to the community, to our places of employment and our church. When we find a buyer we sell the property for $37,000 and we then have made a quick $4,500 in our pocket by just bringing buyer and seller together. The incentive to the other buyer is that he/she is getting a $50,000 property for $37,000 and a cash flow of $200 per month. As you can see everyone here is in a win-win situation. What you have done is flipped the contract to someone else to go to closing because you assigned the contract.

CASH AT CLOSING

This is another very simple concept that if followed, we as believers can use to increase our net worth and build our cash. The same guidelines apply as stated earlier. You can use the same contract for this transaction. The only difference here is you are actually going to close this deal. For example, we will use the same parameters of $50,000 property value and a negotiated sales price of $32,500. Remember, use a promissory note as a down payment (not cash). After about six months to a year go to a bank and refinance. The bank will loan you 80% of the appraised value. 80% of $50,000 is $40,000 minus closing cost. Let's say closing cost is about $2,000; you will walk away with $38,000 - $32,500 = $5,500 in your pocket plus $200 cash flow per month. If we did just two deals per year we could increase our cash to $11,000 and $4,800 per year in income for a yearly total of $15,800 per year. Just think, if we did this for five years we could make $55,000 in cash and $24,000 in cash flow for a total of $79,000 (owning 10 properties). This can be a great retirement vehicle for your family as well (10 properties @ 200 cash flow = $2,000 per month income).

FLIPPING PROPERTIES (FORECLOSURES)

This concept is unique because it only involves purchasing the properties, fixing them and reselling them. The whole concept is to purchase 30 to 40% below market value and resell at market value. This concept is used by those of us who do not want to be landlords. You can really find bargains at foreclosure auctions, particularly if the foreclosure is done when the owners have ten years or less to pay on the mortgage. There are many foreclosure auctions where you can find super deals. In addition, go to a bank and ask for their list of REO properties, tell them what you want to do and establish a working relationship with them. Banks are not in business to have an inventory of properties, so you can negotiate with them and get some really good deals. The most important concept of property flipping is to buy low and sell low.

TAX LIENS AND DEEDS

Tax lien certificates are created when a property owner in the municipality does not pay his/her property taxes. The Lord in His infinite wisdom has created within the system a way for the righteous to obtain the possessions of the unrighteous through the confiscation of their unpaid property taxes. Depending on your state, you may be able to get properties for pennies on the dollar within forty-five days to two years. If you live in a tax deed state, when you pay the property taxes you own the property in forty-five days. If you live in a tax lien state the process may take up to two years. However, you cannot lose because when you purchase the lien, the municipality will pay you an interest percentage to use your money. Note: The municipality needs cash to continue to operate. In Baltimore City Maryland you will receive 18% interest on your money. In Baltimore County you will receive 12% interest on your money. If the property owner pays his/her tax bill, you will receive what you paid for the lien plus interest and penalties. In addition, you will also be paid for any legal bills you incurred in the foreclosure process. If the property owner does not redeem, then you hit the jackpot and receive a property for the cost of the taxes. There are more than 3,000 counties in the United States; we as believers need to familiarize ourselves with the rules of the county holding the tax sale. Remember saints, we still need to do our due diligence regarding the property value, the neighborhood and condition of the property before we bid at the tax sale.

PRE-FORECLOSURES

This is the best-hidden secret in the country in terms of super real estate purchase deals. The concept of the pre-foreclosure market is to negotiate with the borrower before the actual foreclosure. Start by going to the courthouse in the county or municipality the property is located in. Then get the list of foreclosures within the last week. Analyze the properties by looking to see what is owed on the property and the property fair market value. I've come across deals where the homeowners owe $30,000 on the mortgage and the home is valued at $150,000. If you come across this situation, it is a win-win because of the enormous profit potential. The first step is to write a letter to contact the homeowner indicating that you are willing to pay what is owed on the mortgage and put some cash in the pocket of the soon-to-be-in-default homeowner. If the homeowner does nothing about his/her situation they will lose their home and their credit report will be severely damaged. If they (homeowners) contact you then you do your due diligence with regard to value, condition, inspection and contract obligation. Consult your attorney to draw up a quit claim deed and proceed with the purchase of the property. I have included a sample letter to the homeowners and an example of a quit claim deed for your benefit.

QUIT CLAIM DEED

That I (we), _____ the undersigned,

for the consideration of $_____ and other valuable considerations, do hereby release, remise and

forever quitclaim unto_____ all

right, title and interest in that certain property situated in _____ County, State of _____

_____, and described as follows:

Dated:_____   _____

                                                Releasor

                                                _____

                                                Releasor

Marcus A. Beasley

ACKNOWLEDGMENT

STATE OF_____

COUNTY OF_____

On this _____ day of _____ 20_____ before me, the

undersigned Notary Public, personally appeared_____

to me known to be the individuals described in and who executed the foregoing instrument, and acknowledged

that he/she (they) executed the same as his/her (their) free act and deed.

My Commission expires _____   _____

                                                                                      Notary Public

PROMISE LAND PROPERTIES LLC

(SAMPLE LETTER FOR PRE-FORECLOSED REAL ESTATE)

AUGUST 12,2003

Dear Homeowner:

This correspondence is being sent to you because your name has appeared on _____ County's listing of delinquent mortgage payments (foreclosures). According to their records, your mortgage payments are extremely past due. Unfortunately, this means you are in grave danger of losing your property. Whatever the reasons or individual circumstances that led to this situation, WE CAN HELP.

We are looking for motivated property owners that are interested in a fast sale to save their credit rating and/or save them money from a forced foreclosure due to the delinquent mortgage payments on their property. Whether you are looking for some fast cash or a fast sale, WE CAN HELP.

If you decide to do nothing about your delinquent payments, these are the possible consequences that you may encounter:

1. Bank forecloses on your property
2. Credit rating reflects foreclosure
3. Difficulty obtaining any credit
4. Losing all payments you put into your property
5. LOSING YOUR PROPERTY

Don't panic. WE CAN HELP, We can make arrangements with you to put money in your pocket and save your money at the same time. We are a Christian Real Estate Group interested in solving problems for homeowners. If this solution is of interest to you please contact John Doe Properties today. Please call (123) 456-7890 OR (123) 456-7880 (CELL). Don't delay; solve your money problems today!

Sincerely,

John Doe

CEO John Doe Properties LLC

CHAPTER 9

LEAVING AN INHERITANCE FOR YOUR CHILDREN'S CHILDREN

When you have fulfilled all that God has called you to do, what will your legacy be? What will you leave for the next generation of your family?

Proverbs 13:22 says, "A good man leaves an inheritance for his children's children." We as believers only associate the inheritance with material possessions. However, we will look at this scripture from a spiritual perspective to add understanding.

SPIRITUAL INHERITANCE

(RIGHTEOUS VS. UNRIGHTEOUS)

To illustrate to you that an inheritance is also spiritual, let's first look at Joshua 9: 6–15, when the Gibeonites deceive Joshua into entering into a covenant with them." Verse 18 of the same chapter tells us that, "the children of Israel smote them not, because the princes of the congregation had sworn unto them by the Lord God of Israel."

As we look at this account in Joshua we realize that although the Gibeonites used trickery for protection God still honored the covenant. Remember, God is a covenant keeping God.

Now, let's go to 2 Samuel 21:1–9; we see here that the Gibeonites are avenged because of the sins of Saul. In verse 1, "David inquired of the Lord and the Lord answered, It is for Saul, and for his bloody house, because he slew the Gibeonites." Remember the covenant with Joshua and the Gibeonites that God had honored. Saul broke the covenant by killing the Gibeonites. Here is the unrighteous inheritance that Saul left for future generations of his family.

David asked the Gibeonites how could he make atonement for the sins of Saul; the Gibeonites answered by saying they wanted seven men of his (Saul's) sons to be delivered unto them. Because of the sins of a father, seven of Saul's grandchildren were killed because of the unrighteous inheritance that Saul had left them.

On the other hand Jonathan (Saul's son) entered into covenant with David. David remembered how Jonathan saved David's life from the hands of his father Saul. When David asked the Gibeonites what would settle the issue with Saul, he remembered Jonathan and spared Jonathan's son. Jonathan left a righteous inheritance for his children's children.

We must understand the best inheritance is righteous and spiritual because sins can be transferred from generation to generation. We often see tragedy after tragedy in the same family and wonder why. The success of your future generations, spiritually and economically, will depend on the decisions you make today. Make sure that you have a relationship with Jesus and teach your children about Jesus. What an awesome and righteous inheritance this will be for your children.

NATURAL INHERITANCE

You not only have to plan in life but you must also plan to die. God says in His word in 2 Kings 20:1, "Set thine house in order, for thou shall die." God was telling Hezekiah that he needed to prepare for death by setting all of his affairs in order. It is critical that we have an estate plan because if we do not we are burdening our children with legal problems, tax consequences, a probate court distributing our assets, legal and administrative fees, and court-appointed legal guardians for our minor children.

The problem is that it costs money for us to die. Upon our death, our tax is 37% ; it increases to 55% and could go as high as 60%. Now that we have worked so hard and long for our life possessions we must make sure that we are passing it to our next generation and not according to what the probate court says. We need to make sure we have:

1. **Last Will and Testament:** This document instructs how all of your property is to be distributed in the event of your death, names the executor for your estate and designates a guardian for your minor children.

2. **Revocable Trust:** This document will allow you to hold title of your assets in the name of a trust. Please consult with an attorney to discuss the best way for you to transfer your assets to your heirs.

CHAPTER 10

WHAT TO DO NEXT

You may be asking what do I do next? How do I get started and where do I start? If you carefully follow these steps, your financial situation will drastically improve even in the famine.. This is what you do:

1. **Develop your financial plan and write it down on paper.**

2. **Pray and ask God to bless your plan in the name of Jesus.**

3. **Visualize your plan manifesting itself in the natural. (We want to develop self-identification mechanism within you creating an attitude.)**

4. **Confess your plan verbally.**

5. **WORK YOUR PLAN.**

6. **Create a budget.**

7. **Stop spending (buy only necessities). Do not buy on credit for eighteen months.**

8. **Track daily, weekly and monthly spending.**

9. **Order your credit report. Look for inaccuracies and contact delinquent account companies.**

10. **Negotiate with creditors if necessary and write letters to credit bureaus.**

11. **Look at your pay to determine if you can give yourself a raise by increasing exemptions.**

12. **Look at income opportunities to bring more money into your home.**

13. **Consider real estate as an option to increase cash flow.**

14. **Make sure you have medical coverage, proper life insurance, disability insurance, emergency fund, college planning, long-term care insurance and retirement planning.**

15. **Create a will or a revocable trust. Consult with an estate planning attorney**

16. **If you do all of the things listed here you are showing God that you have faith in Him because of your works. God will bless you because He said in Proverbs, "If you choose the path I will guide your footsteps."**

GOD BLESS YOU AND YOUR FAMILY

CHAPTER 11

MY TESTIMONY

In 1999 I married the beautiful Denise French and my life was never the same. God says in His word, "When a man finds a wife he finds a good thing and obtains favor from the Lord." Denise and I immediately set goals and were determined to obtain financial independence and live the quality lifestyle God has promised in His word.

In 2000–2001 we decided to eliminate our debts and restore our credit report. In making this decision we knew we could not buy anything on credit and we decided to go over our budget and stop spending in the areas we deemed excessive. This continued for two years. In 2002 we had eliminated twelve debts and my credit score increased from 580 to 720.

In March 2002 my wife approached me and suggested that we should go to the Baltimore County Tax Sale. My reply to her was "I don't think that is such a good idea." My wife was determined and she printed a copy of the properties to be auctioned and brought it home to me. I looked over the list and at that moment the Holy Spirit spoke to me and said, "Look over this list and see what properties have over $5,000 in back taxes with very little or no mortgage." Of course I was obedient and did exactly what I was told. To my surprise I found one property in particular that fit the description the Holy Spirit gave to me. I told my wife about what the Holy Spirit told me and we decided to go and look at the property. The property was in a growing area of the county called Owings Mills. After completing our due diligence on the property we decided to attend the auction on June 4 and bid.

On June 4, I attended the auction and saw maybe 50 people at the auction. I was disappointed because so many people were in attendance. However, the Lord reminded me that I can do all things through Christ that strengthens me. The auction started and there were about five guys bidding and buying all of the properties. I asked another guy in attendance about these five individuals. He told me they were millionaires and they did this every year. My confidence was shaken after hearing this piece of information. God, however, continued to remind me about His word when he said, "The king's heart is in my hands and I turn whatsoever way I please." I then grew stronger in my faith in the Lord at that moment. As the auction progressed these same five guys were bidding against each other to buy the properties. One hour had passed and only one other person was able to win a bid other than the five millionaires. The auction was only 2 properties from the property I wanted to bid on. Just before the property I wanted to bid on came up, the auctioneer said, "If anyone wants to come up and tell why they want this property come on up." The Spirit said to me, "Go up and say you want this property for the kingdom of the Lord." I was again obedient and did exactly that. The Lord quieted the mouths of the millionaires and I was awarded the property for $5,569. Once again God has shown Himself faithful.

Maryland is a tax lien state so the property owner has up to six months to redeem his/her property. My wife and I began to pray to gain ownership of this property. I spoke to attorneys, friends and associates and they all indicated only about 1% of the people did not redeem and so we would not come to own this property. Of course we did not receive this in our Spirits. We spoke those things that be not as though they were. I began to call the tax line almost daily to see if the owner had paid the delinquent taxes. God one day spoke to me and said," Why are you calling every day? Do you not trust me?" I replied yes I do. The Lord reminded me how He allowed me to win the bid in the first place. God then said to me," Do not call any more until the time I tell you to call." It was difficult for me but I was obedient. I did not call for four months. At this point the six-month redemption period had expired so we began the foreclosure process. The owner still can redeem the property during this period but he/she must pay, in addition to taxes, legal expenses as well. The foreclosure process took about six months and on June 11, 2003 we were awarded the property. What a blessing that God had given to us.

In January 2003, God had also impressed upon my heart to buy a two-unit apartment building. We closed on this building and walked away from the settlement table with over $20,000 in cash.

In August we decided to refinance our tax lien property. Little did we know the spiritual warfare we were about to face. We started on the 22nd of August. We applied with the largest lender in the country. At first things seemed to be going nicely. We got a credit approval in two days. After the credit approval things began to progress in the negative direction. The first issue was regarding the title. My name was not on the title for six weeks because the county just overlooked my file. This delayed my loan for almost four weeks. The second issue was non-owner-occupied status. The appraiser had indicated on his report that the property was vacant. At this point the lender declined my loan. The good news was that we bought a property from the tax sale for $5,569 and the property appraised for almost $200,000. We then changed the status to occupied and resubmitted the loan. The third issue was that we needed a phone bill to show that we were going to occupy the property. We produced the phone service to satisfy the requirement. The fourth issue was again the title issue. We finally satisfied this requirement by personally going to the county and demanding the change be made. The fifth issue was my debt ratio and our other properties we owned. This took about two more weeks to satisfy. The sixth issue was again the phone bill. We felt we had finally conquered all of the obstacles but we were sadly mistaken. We continued to pray and ask God to assist us day after day for eighty days. The lender finally gave us an approval but we had one final showdown with the enemy. We soon learned thereafter that the title company decided that they were not going to insure the title because they could not understand how anybody could get a property for $5,569 which was worth almost $200,000. We soon realized that the world could not understand what God had done and the world wanted to shut the door. However, when the world shuts the door God opens a window. We had our attorney call the title company but the title company completely refused to have any conversation with our attorney. We then had our attorney call the lender and indicate to them that he could insure the title for the loan. The lender did not want a title company they were not familiar with, so the original title company decided to insure the title.

On Monday November 17, the day our credit line was to be funded, the lender decided not to have the proceeds distributed to us. How bizarre is that? We went in fervent prayer against the enemy. By the end of the day we went forward with the distribution.

On April 25, 2003 God entrusted us with His most prized possession, Christian Elijah D'Angelo Beasley. He was a blessing because we were in prayer for three years awaiting his arrival.

Remember, God has no respect of persons; if he did it for me he can and will do it for you.

SEMINARS & CONFERENCES

If your organization or church is interested in seminars or conferences, we have two that we teach:

1. ECONOMIC EMPOWERMENT—This seminar focuses on planning, faith, programming, education & implementation of spiritual and natural laws of finance . The topics we teach include:

    a) Debt and credit strategies

    b) Investment strategies

    c) Income opportunities

    d) Emergency fund preparation

    e) College fund preparation

    f) Insurance protection

    g) Retirement planning strategies

    h) Estate planning strategies

    i) Long-term care preparation

2. POSSESSING THE PROMISED LAND- This seminar focuses on the wealth transference to the saints. This is a real estate seminar that will give many unknown strategies to possess the land by force. The topics include

a) Flipping contracts for $3 to $5,000 per contract.

b) Flipping properties without using your own money or credit

c) Cash at closing without using any money or credit

d) Buying bank foreclosed property.

e) Tax sale opportunities that could make you debt-free in less than two years

f) Foreclosure and pre-foreclosure hidden treasures in your town or county

If you or your organization is interested in any of these seminars please contact Marcus A. Beasley at 1-800-892-5558 ext. 88288.

BIBLIOGRAPHY

Larry Burkett, *The Coming Economic Earthquake* (1991)

David D'Arcangelo, *Wealth Starts at Home* (1997)

Dale Hanson Bourke, *The Passages of Life Bible* (1995)

Holy Bible, *King James Version* (1973)

William MacDonald, *Bible Commentary* (1997)

William C. Martin, *Laymen's Bible* (1964)

About The Author

Marcus A. Beasley was born in Beaufort South Carolina in 1963. Marcus graduated from Baptist College in 1985. He is currently a Financial Advisor for AIG/Valic in Baltimore Maryland.

God spoke to Marcus in 2003 in the midst of an economic famine and inspired him to write His (God's) plan of economic prosperity in the midst of a famine. God's plan includes spiritual and natural applications that if used will economically prosper His people whatever the current economic condition.

www.ingramcontent.com/pod-product-compliance
Lightning Source LLC
Chambersburg PA
CBHW080424290526
45791CB00008BA/2398